www.wadsworth.com

wadsworth.com is the World Wide Web site for Wadsworth Publishing Company and is your direct source to dozens of online resources.

At *wadsworth.com* you can find out about supplements, demonstration software, and student resources. You can also send e-mail to many of our authors and preview new publications and exciting new technologies.

wadsworth.com
Changing the way the world learns®

ONLINE EDUCATION

Learning and Teaching in Cyberspace

Greg Kearsley

Wadsworth
Thomson Learning

Australia • Canada • Mexico • Singapore • Spain • United Kingdom • United States

Education Editor: *Dianne Lindsay*
Assistant Editor: *Tangelique Williams*
Editorial Assistant: *Keynia Johnson*
Marketing Manager: *Becky Tollerson*
Project Editor: *Trudy Brown*
Print Buyer: *Mary Noel*
Permissions Editor: *Joohee Lee*

Production Service: *Scratchgravel Publishing Services*
Text Designer: *Anne Draus*
Copy Editor: *Margaret Tropp*
Cover Designer: *Laurie Anderson*
Cover Printer: *Webcom, Ltd.*
Compositor: *Scratchgravel Publishing Services*
Printer: *Webcom, Ltd.*

Library of Congress Cataloging-in-Publication Data
Kearsley, Greg, [date]–
   Online education : learning and teaching in cyberspace / Greg Kearsley.
      p. cm.
   Includes bibliographical references (p.) and index.
   ISBN 0-534-50689-5 (alk. paper)
   1. Computer-assisted instruction.   2. Education—Data processing.   I. Title.

LB1028.5 .K35   2000
371.33'4—dc21   99-052303

For more information, contact
Wadsworth/Thomson Learning
10 Davis Drive
Belmont, CA 94002-3098
USA
http://www.wadsworth.com

International Headquarters
Thomson Learning
International Division
290 Harbor Drive, 2nd Floor
Stamford, CT 06902-7477
USA

UK/Europe/Middle East/South Africa
Thomson Learning
Berkshire House
168-173 High Holborn
London WC1V 7AA
United Kingdom

Asia
Thomson Learning
60 Albert Street, #15-01
Albert Complex
Singapore 189969

Canada
Nelson Thomson Learning
1120 Birchmount Road
Toronto, Ontario M1K 5G4
Canada

Contents

3 Elements of Online Education 27

4 Research about Online Education 45

5 Online Learning 61

6 Online Teaching   77

7 Design and Development of Online Courses   93

8 Organizations and Networking   108

Preface

Cyberspace. A consensual hallucination experienced daily by billions of legitimate operators in every nation, by children being taught mathematical concepts. . . . A graphical representation of data abstracted from the banks of every computer in the human system. Unthinkable complexity.
(Gibson, 1984, p. 51)

This book is about what happens when cyberspace becomes a reality and how it will change the way we learn and teach. Although the book is primarily concerned with formal education (courses/classes offered by schools and colleges), it is impossible to ignore the fact that much online learning takes place outside this setting. Indeed, part of the fundamental change that computer networks are bringing about in education is blurring the lines between formal and informal learning. When students do their learning at home, from the office, in the evening, or on the weekend, is it school or not? And does it matter?

Although you will find plenty of discussion herein about all aspects of online learning and teaching, you won't find much about the actual technology of networks. The technical details of how a network operates are basically irrelevant to how it is used. It is true that these details affect how much and what kind of information can be carried, which in turn affect the nature of the interaction possible, but these are constraints on usage, not a determining factor. Equally important, network technology changes at such an astonishing pace that trying to describe it in a book is largely self-defeating. (However, some relevant links are provided on this book's Web site.)

Thus, *Online Education* simply assumes that networks exist and takes it from there. Indeed, networks have become the backbone of modern society, the global and local infrastructure that allows us to function—the well-worn information highway (and back roads) metaphor. Networks affect just about every daily action we perform, from making telephone calls to shopping for groceries to walking the dog (the stoplights at intersections are likely to be tied into traffic control systems). And they will come to play a dominant role in all aspects of learning.

The most amazing thing is that we are just at the very beginning of the network age. The kinds of capabilities and forms of interaction possible with computer systems in the coming decades will make our current uses seem incredibly primitive. Yet even now we are having trouble understanding how to change our education system to take advantage of the simple capabilities we already have. It is difficult to see how we will make the transition from here to there. But then, human beings have always demonstrated remarkable adaptability as a species and as individuals. So, cyberspace, here we come.

Audience and Scope

This book is intended primarily for existing and prospective teachers who want to understand what online education is all about. As such, it will be useful as a textbook for preservice courses in Schools of Education as well as in-service workshops conducted by school and college systems. The book should also be useful to administrators or managers responsible for planning and implementing online education programs. In addition, the book should be helpful to anyone who is about to engage in online learning and wants an idea of what to expect.

The book assumes that readers have some basic familiarity with computer concepts and applications. However, it is not a book about computers, and it doesn't require any significant technical background. It is a book about teaching and learning, so the more you know about these subjects, the more you will find it useful.

Note that this is not a "how-to" book that explains how to develop online courses, hook up computers to the Internet, or decide what kinds of online applications to use in your teaching. But it does provide the conceptual basis needed for such tasks and a good understanding of the underlying issues. Acquiring a broader understanding will result in more effective online teaching and learning.

The Web Site

The Web site for this book, at **http://home.sprynet.com/~gkearsley/cyber.htm,** contains direct links to all the sites mentioned in the book, as well as others. It also provides a discussion forum where individuals or classes can post their views about online education and share their experiences firsthand.

Organization of the Book

The book begins with an introductory chapter that outlines some of the major themes of online education and provides a tour of Web sites that illustrate these themes. Indeed, Web sites are used throughout the book as specific examples; the upside of this is that you can visit the sites directly if you want more detail. The downside is that Web sites come and go, and some of the links may be deceased by the time you read this book. (Check the book Web site for the most current links.)

Chapter 2 outlines the scope of online education across different learning settings: higher education, K–12 schools, corporations and government agencies, nonprofit organizations, the home, and public spaces. Chapter 3 discusses the basic elements of online education: email, threaded discussions, real-time conferencing, groupware, file transfer, application programs, and simulation. The chapter concludes with an overview of tools for online curriculum development and management—a topic that is addressed further in Chapter 7. Chapter 4 covers research about online education: student achievement, evaluation of Web-based courses, school-level impact, nature of class interaction, and virtual conferences.

Chapter 5 examines critical aspects of online learning: learning to learn, the social milieu, engagement, netiquette, and special needs. Topics covered in Chapter 6, on online teaching, include interactivity and participation, feedback, moderating and facilitating, effectiveness, workload, and faculty collaboration. Chapter 7 discusses the design and development of online courses: methodology, form and function, team approach, course documents, integrating online and on-campus activities, and authoring.

The subsequent three chapters deal with a variety of issues, including organizations (Chapter 8), policy (Chapter 9), and societal impact (Chapter 10). These issues determine the success or failure of online education in specific settings or overall. Chapter 11 addresses some of the practical issues encountered in the implementation of online courses. Chapter 12 offers some speculation about the future directions of online education, and Chapter 13 lists sources of further information. The Appendix provides case studies of online courses, programs, and learning events, and the Glossary defines the key terms used in the book.

At the end of each chapter is a set of questions "for further reflection"; these questions can be used for class discussions, assignments, or projects.

Throughout the book, you will find brief introductions to key individuals in the field of online education, including links to their work. These links allow you to check out directly the ideas of those who are shaping cyberspace.

Acknowledgments

A book like this depends on the help and generosity of many people. I want to thank my editor at Wadsworth/Thomson Learning, Dianne Lindsay, for seeing the project through. I also want to thank the University of Wisconsin for the use of its library system on those occasions when I needed to read an actual book or journal. Finally, I want to acknowledge the role of the reviewers in making this a better work through their incisive comments on initial drafts: Terry Anderson, University of Alberta; Robert Gillan, Northwestern State University of Louisiana; Liza Greenberg, University of Miami; Charlotte N. Gunawardena, University of New Mexico; Regina Halpin, Mississippi State University; Douglas E. Hansen, Saginaw Valley State University; Robert G. Main, California State University, Chico; LeAnn McKinzie, West Texas A & M University; Richard J. O'Connor, University of Arkansas, Monticello; Andrew Torok, Northern Illinois University; and Terry Weeks, Middle Tennessee State University.

Greg Kearsley

1

Introduction

After completing this chapter, you should understand:

- the relationship between past work in computer-assisted or computer-based instruction (CAI/CBI) and contemporary online education

- the major themes that characterize online education

- how online learning differs from traditional classroom instruction

Welcome to the 21st century. You are a Netizen (a Net Citizen), and you exist as a citizen of the world thanks to the global connectivity that the Net makes possible. You consider everyone as your compatriot. You physically live in one country but you are in contact with much of the world via the global computer network. Virtually, you live next door to every other single Netizen in the world. Geographical separation is replaced by existence in some virtual space. (Hauben & Hauben, 1997, p. 3)

As the opening quote suggests, the 21st century will be one in which society is dramatically transformed by computer networks. The way we live, how we work, what people do for entertainment, and the nature of human relationships are likely to change significantly (Benedikt, 1991; Jones, 1995; Whittle, 1997). Although these changes have already begun, they are nothing compared to what lies ahead.

The world of education will be very different: what students and teachers do, when and where learning takes place, the nature of educational experiences. Schooling, as we know it, will change dramatically; almost everyone will become a lifelong learner, continually engaged in some form of learning activity, either formal or casual.

This book is about how we get from here to there. Most aspects of online education already exist, and in some cases have been in use for a number of years. We have a lot of research findings and practical experience. It's just a matter of connecting the dots to see the whole picture.

The History of Computers in Education

One thing that is not very helpful in understanding online education is the way computers have been used in the past for learning applications. This history goes back about four decades and is usually referred to as computer-assisted instruction (CAI) or computer-based instruction (CBI) (see Allessi & Trollip, 1991, or Gibbons & Fairweather, 1998). Although CAI/CBI covered a lot of ground (including some forms that are quite worthwhile, such as simulations and thinking tools), the overall philosophy focused on electronic curriculum materials—programs that students could interact with to learn specific content. The main idea was that computers could provide individualized learning experiences, including interactive sequences consisting of problems or questions with appropriate feedback. All of this rested upon a sound theoretical basis of behavioral and early cognitive learning theory. And there was ample empirical evidence to show that it worked in terms of student achievement scores or learning outcomes.

But it became clear over time that although this approach may have some limited value, it is not a very powerful way to use computers in education. Instead we realized that computers are superb devices for communication and information sharing. What really impressed students and teachers was the capability to interact electronically and search through databases (Fisher, Dwyer, & Yokam, 1996; Kearsley, Hunter, & Furlong, 1992; Maddux, Johnson, & Willis, 1997). So, interactivity was very important, but not the kind of interaction originally conceived of in CAI/CBI.

Actually the evidence for this had been there all along, but it took a while to sink in. One of the largest CAI/CBI systems of its time, PLATO, had an email system (called p-notes), which was used more than the "courseware" provided. Bulletin board systems and early networks such as Bitnet, FIDOnet, and Arpanet, were very popular with all levels of users—from high school students to university researchers. And early work with computer-mediated conferencing (CMC) systems showed that students had very meaningful educational experiences using them (for example, Hiltz & Turoff, 1993).

But it wasn't till the World Wide Web (aka the "Web") appeared in the early 1990s that this all became clear. The Web makes it very easy to create and access networked information. It also brings together all major forms of inter-

Seymour Papert: Liberating Young Minds

An interesting slice of the history of educational computing can be viewed through the work of Seymour Papert, long associated with MIT. His early contribution to the field of education was the development and proselytizing of the LOGO programming language (see Papert, 1980). The concept underlying LOGO was to provide children with a way to explore ideas by writing computer programs and to put them in control of the computer rather than vice versa. His later work has focused on computer games and the role of computer activities in family settings (for example, Papert, 1993, 1996). Papert's work has played a pivotal role in changing education because he has continually focused on the role of technology as tools to be used by children in their intellectual development. In doing so, he provided a counterpoint to the prevailing views of CAI/CBI and ultimately pushed the field in different directions.

To learn more about Papert, see his MIT home page at http://papert.www.media.mit.edu/people/papert. Or see the Connected Family site at http://www.ConnectedFamily.com.

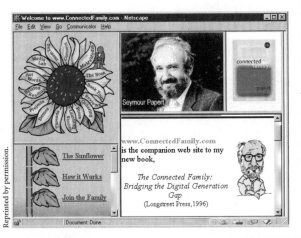

personal interaction such as email, chats, threaded discussions, and conferencing. Plus, it adds multimedia (graphics, sound, video) to the equation. The Web even supports "classic" forms of CAI/CBI such as drills or tutorials, should anyone want to do that kind of thing (old habits die out slowly).

Themes That Shape Online Education

Given that the history of educational computing isn't very useful in understanding the current situation, let's spend the rest of this chapter on a tour of Web sites that provide better clues. Actually, we will be looking at Web sites throughout the book, but those cited in this chapter are more general in nature than those included in subsequent chapters. Of course, the best way to appreciate these sites is to go exploring them yourself—and you are encouraged to do so at any time! (Remember, the book Web site provides "hot" links.)

In the following tour, we will examine a number of themes that shape online education—and the future direction of learning and teaching. Note that although we will discuss each of these themes separately, they are all interrelated and overlapping.

The Global SchoolNet Foundation (http://www.gsn.org) is dedicated to creating interaction among kids around the world. It is based upon the FrEd mail system, an early email system for students and educators.

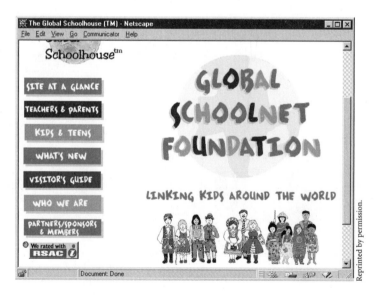

Collaboration

Without any doubt, the biggest single change that online education brings about is an increased tendency toward collaboration among students and teachers. Many online projects involve information-sharing activities between classes located in different places. Even when there is no specific intent to collaborate, it often happens anyway because it is so easy to interact online. This type of interaction stands in contrast to the traditional model of schools in which each classroom is a self-contained and isolated unit. Collaboration may involve pairs of students, small groups, or entire classes.

Connectivity

Online education provides wide-ranging connectivity. Students can easily connect with each other and their instructors through email and conferencing. Students can also connect easily with parents, as many students away at college do ("Dad/Mom: Please send more money"). Even more impressive is that students can interact directly with experts in their field of study. Anyone who knows how to use an online address directory (such as 411.com) can track down someone's email address. Indeed, many educational projects have been set up to put students and experts in contact and foster a dialog.

The Jason Project (http://www.jasonproject.org) gives students all over the world a chance to participate directly in scientific projects led by Dr. Robert Ballard.

Reprinted by permission.

Student-Centeredness

Another common characteristic of online education is that it is student-centered. Although teachers and faculty still play a key role in creating and organizing a class, students largely determine its direction by virtue of their participation and activities. Instructors define the goals and facilitate or manage the learning process; students discover the content on their own and carry out assignments or projects. This means that online courses are often less structured (more chaotic?) than traditional classes. It also means that students must accept more self-responsibility for their learning.

Unboundedness

It is often said that online education eliminates the walls of the classroom, in the sense that it gives students access to information and people anywhere in the world. At the same time, it opens up the classroom to many additional students. Online education removes boundaries having to do with where and when students learn, as well as who can be a learner. It is a great boon to individuals who live in remote places, who are disabled, who relocate frequently, or who are somehow different from "typical" students enrolled in a program of study.

This consideration is especially important in the workplace, where it may too costly or time-consuming for employees to attend training courses. With online education, people can learn things at the job site or at home, without the need to go off to a training program at some distant location. Furthermore, they can learn as much or as little as they need to—unlike traditional training programs that come in "one size fits all" courses.

MayaQuest was the first of a series of ongoing interactive expeditions, involving thousands of students, available at the Classroom Connect site (http://www.classroom.com).

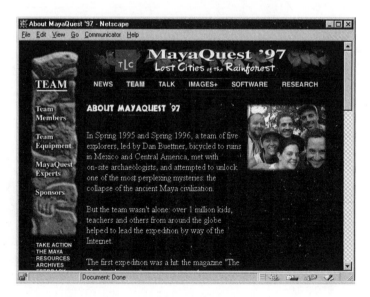

Community

Education takes place in a community, whether it is the community of learning defined by a particular school or college, or a physical community such as a town or city. Online education can bring together any community by increasing accessibility and connectivity. The simple step of creating a home page on the Web that provides links to previously separate elements, or an online directory with email or telephone numbers, helps to establish a community.

Indeed, computer networks make it possible to define virtual communities that unite people around common interests (see Rheingold, 1993). A Web site for dog lovers or wine connoisseurs creates a virtual community that does not correspond to any physical location. It is possible to create a virtual school or college that consists of a learning community with no actual buildings. Some people may be uncomfortable with this concept, but it is just a fact of cyberspace.

Blacksburg Electronic Village (http://www.bev.net): A college town becomes one of the country's first wired communities.

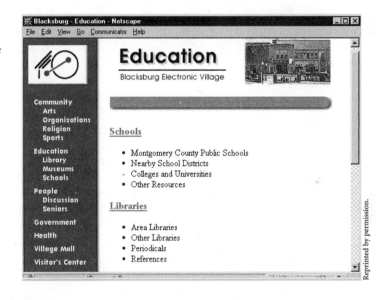

Exploration

Many online activities involve some sort of adventure or discovery learning format. If computer games can be so much fun, why shouldn't "serious" learning be fun too? Young children, in particular, love to explore, and online classes in K–8 often use this approach. It is also a good format for museums and science centers, where people go to be entertained as well as enlightened.

A more formal type of exploration is problem-based learning, which is commonly used in professional education (law, medicine, engineering, business). In this approach, students are given problem situations or case studies and asked to work out a solution, diagnosis, strategy, or design. Problem-based learning is very compatible with online education because access to resources and expertise is a key aspect of problem solving.

The San Francisco Exploratorium (http://www.exploratorium.edu) is an online museum that offers plenty of interesting activities.

Shared Knowledge

Although the sharing of knowledge is at the core of education, we have only been able to share in limited ways prior to computer networks. Books are obviously a wonderful technology for sharing knowledge—relatively inexpensive, highly portable, and long-lasting. But only a tiny fraction of human knowledge gets published, and a bookshelf or library can hold only a fraction

Many government agencies, like the U.S. Geological Survey, offer educationally oriented Web pages (http://info.er.usgs.gov).

of that. Putting information on the Web (or some other electronic format) makes it immediately available to anyone in the world with a suitable computer connection. Everyone can be an author/publisher (for better or for worse).

Students can tap into this vast shared knowledge network for schoolwork, and they can contribute to it as well. Indeed, the Web does not distinguish between documents created by Nobel laureates and fifth graders. What matters is the quality and usefulness of the information provided.

Multisensory Experience

We know that learning is more effective when it involves multiple sensory channels (visuals, color, movement, sounds, voice, touch, smell). We also know that individuals have different sensory preferences (called cognitive styles). Multimedia technology (much of which is available via the Web) can provide certain kinds of multisensory learning experiences. Although these interactions are not as rich or complete as firsthand experiences (for example, no touch or smell), they are often much better than traditional classroom learning activities based on "talk and chalk."

Video has become a pivotal aspect of networks because it allows people to have face-to-face contact, whether in real-time videoconferences or prerecorded segments. Video is the link between the familiar world of television and the newer domain of computing. Information provided in video format is much richer than text and allows computer interaction to come closer to in-person contact.

The Mt. Diablo Multimedia Academy has produced the Digital Safari (http://intergate. cccoe.k12.ca.us/ mdtech), an example of how schools are embracing multimedia technology.

The Math Forum (http://forum.swarthmore.edu) is a source of mathematics help and information provided by the faculty and students at Swarthmore College.

Authenticity

One of the correlates of connectivity, community, and shared knowledge is that online education is highly authentic in nature. Ironically, the virtual world can be more real than the actual classroom. Because students can access actual databases and experts, their learning activities are realistic. The lack of realism in traditional instruction has often been identified as a major weakness of education at all levels. Indeed, one of the reasons that students often give for disillusionment with school or college is that it lacks "real-world" relevance.

The Web provides direct access to major repositories of research information such as government agencies and clearinghouses. Almost every corporation has a Web page that provides details about its current and future business interests. And increasingly, the world's technical literature, as represented by journal articles and conference proceedings, is available online.

The Brave New World

The nine themes just discussed illustrate some of the major ways in which online education differs from traditional classroom instruction. To be sure, some of these elements do show up in classrooms occasionally, and they could be practiced more in that setting if we wanted. But, taken together, these elements define a new way of learning and teaching that is fundamen-

Some countries have made the support of online education a national priority—for example, Canada's SchoolNet (http://www.schoolnet.ca).

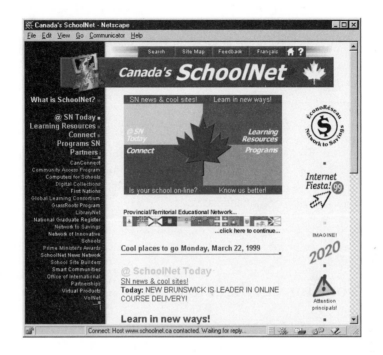

tally different from what we currently do in schools. In the rest of this book, we will examine what this means in detail—for students, teachers, educational institutions, and society in general.

When introduced to the idea of online education, many people assume that it means some kind of impersonal, mechanistic context. The great irony is that online education is much more humane and personal than most forms of classroom instruction. Online education involves levels of connectivity, community, and knowledge sharing that are rarely seen in school settings. However, online learning and teaching are quite different in nature from traditional formats, and this creates uncertainty and discomfort. For most students and teachers, it's something quite new and takes a little while to get used to. Because it represents major changes in the way education is designed and delivered, it will pose big challenges for the administrators and managers who try to implement it in their institutions and organizations.

Because online education is a brave new world, we don't know where it will take us. We don't even know how to do it very well yet. But it is clearly an imperative, not an option. As technology races ahead at breakneck speed, transforming our lives, we need a way to keep up with it, to stay in control. The world is changing too quickly and there is too much information for our old methods of instruction to work any longer. We need to embrace online education for our personal and collective well-being.

For further discussions about the impact of telecommunications on learning, see Benson and Fodemski (1996), Collis (1996), Duning, Van Kererix, and Zabrowski (1993), or Schrum and Berenfeld (1997).

Key Ideas

- Online education is very different from the early uses of computers for teaching and learning (CAI/CBI).
- Nine themes that characterize online education are (1) collaboration, (2) connectivity, (3) student-centeredness, (4) unboundedness, (5) community, (6) exploration, (7) shared knowledge, (8) multisensory experience, and (9) authenticity.
- Online education requires new forms of teaching and learning compared to traditional classroom instruction.

Questions for Further Reflection

1. Research the CAI/CBI literature. Why do you think that interaction between a program and a person became the dominant idea of this approach?
2. Are there important positive aspects of traditional classroom instruction that are not going to be part of online education? How about negative aspects?
3. As a student, what do you feel is the most difficult aspect of online education? How about for a teacher?
4. Of the different themes discussed in this chapter, which one seems the most significant to you in terms of changing the nature of education?
5. Imagine that you are in a leadership position in education, such as a school principal or a college president (or maybe you are!). What concerns would you have about introducing online education in your institution?
6. Investigate what different countries are doing in online education. Compare their approaches.

2

Scope of
Online Education

After completing this chapter, you should understand

- the network infrastructure required for online education

- the different forms that online learning and teaching take across different levels of the education system

Education has changed from an orderly world of disciplines and courses to an infosphere in which communication technologies are increasingly important. While education is changing, it is not changing fast enough. It is clear that in the future we will see a major restructuring of our social, industrial and educational institutions, and an increased reliance on computers and telecommunications for work and education. (Molnar, 1997, p. 68)

Exactly what is online education? The first chapter discussed nine major characteristics that help to define it. But it is even more diverse in nature than these characteristics would indicate. In this chapter, we examine the many different types and levels of online education. And even though we discuss each category separately, in reality they are interrelated and interconnected in cyberspace.

Networks

Obviously, online education involves the use of computer networks for learning and teaching. However, these may include large-scale public networks such as the Internet or small local area networks (LANs) in a specific building. The latter may be the basis for an electronic classroom or a campus/ school computing system. In most institutions and organizations, LANs are connected to public networks, making the distinction transparent to individual users.

The Consortium for School Networking (CoSN) is a good source of information about educational networks (http://www.cosn.org).

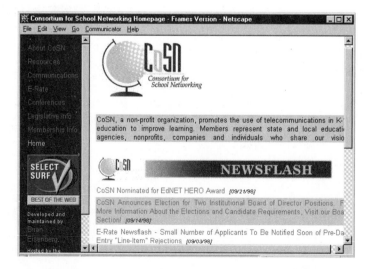

Connections to public networks are usually made through modems and regular telephone lines, whereas LAN connections involve direct connections via cable. School and college systems with many locations in a region or state are likely to lease high-speed data communication lines using fiber optics or microwave transmission. Large corporations and government/military agencies tend to rely on satellites for data transmission and their network communications. It is also possible (and increasingly common) for people to connect to public networks or LANs via wireless means such as cellular or packet radio.

Any kind of network use requires considerable technology infrastructure: hardware, software, and most of all, support personnel. Luckily, most educators need little understanding of infrastructure to engage in online teaching, but administrators do have to understand some basics in order to build, operate, and maintain networks. The aspect of networks that everyone (including students) does have to deal with is getting connected. For most individuals, this means obtaining an account with an Internet service provider (ISP) and perhaps choosing the type of connection (such as cable modem, ISDN, or regular phone line). For educational institutions, it means obtaining enough phone lines or high-speed data connections to provide sufficient access to public networks for their students and staff. It also means providing enough LAN connections in classrooms and offices to meet the need for communication within the institution.

Most U.S. government agencies, corporations, and postsecondary institutions invest a significant amount of their resources in network development and support (for example, Gascoyne & Ozcubucku, 1996; Martin,

Web66, hosted by the University of Minnesota (http://web66.coled.umn.edu), is a Web site intended to help schools get online.

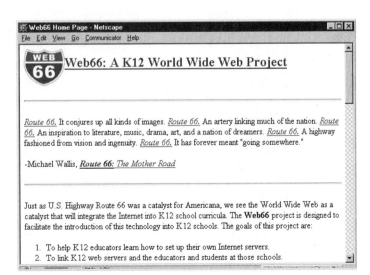

1996). However, until recently, schools did not. But in the late 1990s federal and state governments, driven by the White House and state governors, launched a tremendous effort to develop network infrastructure throughout the U.S. public school system. This initiative involved large grants to school systems, the creation of a telecommunications subsidy (the E-rate), and many partnerships between telecommunications companies and schools. At the same time, new high-speed network technology (such as Internet 2) was being implemented. By the dawn of the 21st century, the network infrastructure of the United States and most other developed nations was ready for online education. (Alas, teachers, administrators, and parents were not—but more about this later in the book.)

Higher Education

Without a doubt, online education is most extensive at universities and colleges, especially at the graduate level. This popularity is mostly due to the easy availability of computers and networks (remember the Internet began as a research network among universities). However, it is also due to the presence of mature, motivated students capable of the independent study required in many online courses, and faculty familiar enough with network applications (such as email and the Web) to offer such courses. The presence of good technical support in terms of computer software, networks, and instructional development is also a major factor.

Online courses developed and used at universities and colleges tend to take the form of Web-based databases for the subject domains in which faculty are experts. They usually include lecture notes, links to relevant sites, and online articles/readings. The courses are also likely to include threaded discussion forums or real-time conferencing capabilities (see next chapter). They may be used as supplements to existing on-campus classes or as stand-alone offerings that involve no on-campus aspects at all.

At first, online courses are usually developed on the initiative of individual faculty, but eventually an entire program or college goes online. At this point, many additional features are usually added to the Web site, including course schedules, administrative information, student grades, placement, and alumni activities. Responsibility for Web development and maintenance, as well as document formats, becomes formalized.

Another common development is for faculty at different institutions to work together to create a Web site for use by their students, or perhaps the public in general. In some cases, this is an informal collaboration between two or three faculty members; in other cases, it may be a formal consortium

The Charles Dickens Web site created by Mitsuharu Matsuoka at Nagoya University, Japan (http://www.lang.nagoyau.ac.jp/~matsuoka/Dickens.html).

with dozens of members. Such collaborations have long been common in academia, but the Web makes the results of the efforts (curriculum materials, research reports, databases) much easier for participants and outsiders to access.

It is difficult to estimate what percentage of courses in higher education are currently in online form, because they may involve many different formats. For example, an on-campus course may use email for interaction

GASNet (Global Anesthesiology Server Network) is an example of a cross-institutional site for medical education hosted by Yale University (http://gasnet.med.yale.edu).

outside of class sessions, or have networked lab activities, but otherwise be a traditional course. However, there is a clear trend for more and more college courses to be offered completely in online form, with no on-campus component.

The American School Directory site (http://www.asd.com) provides links to more than 70,000 schools in the United States. It is designed as a school selection tool, and its alumni page also provides a way for students to stay in touch after graduation.

K–12 Schools

For K–12 schools, the major value of the Internet is to provide a gigantic online library system. Students and teachers are no longer limited by the confines of a single textbook or a small library collection, but can seek out information just about anywhere. Furthermore, finding information online is more like a field trip than a visit to the library, because the sites visited are often very rich in details. Indeed, electronic field trips to the Web sites of museums, zoos, foreign countries, government agencies (such as NASA), and even the White House, have become a popular U.S. classroom activity.

Another very popular application of networks at the K–12 level is undertaking collaborative projects, either within a single class or across multiple schools. Students are organized into small groups, each with a project topic, then use networks to collect relevant information and prepare a report or presentation. The network aspects may involve a LAN within a school that accesses CD-ROMs, or more likely, accessing the Web via the Internet. Many of these projects involve interaction with students at other schools via email, often in an international context. For example, students might be teamed up with those at another school in a foreign country and given the assignment to collect demographic information from each other, such as population, number of churches or hospitals, and other statistics. A number of online Web sites facilitate this kind of interaction, including the Epals Classroom Exchange (http://www.epals.com), which has connected more than 10,000 classrooms in more than 100 different countries.

Even a simple project such as this allows students to deal with language and cultural considerations, as well as social issues raised by demographic differences. It is also possible to develop math skills in the way the information collected is analyzed and presented (great opportunities for percentages and graphs) or to pursue interesting science themes (such as the ecology or chemistry of pollution). And there are always plenty of opportunities for exchange of ideas about art and music, either historic or contemporary.

The sophistication and complexity of these information-sharing projects can vary enormously across grade levels and schools. At the elementary level, the exchanges tend to be limited to "email pals," with students trading messages about favorite topics and practicing their language/writing skills. In the middle grades, the projects tend to be structured around curricular studies in areas such as geography, history, politics, and science. At the high school level, students are encouraged to conduct projects of personal interest related to subject areas they want to explore in more depth. It is not uncommon for

The Science Learning Network (http://www.sln.org) provides access to collaborative science projects.

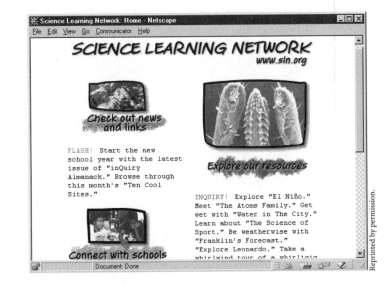

The East/West project in Canada involved the collaboration of four provinces to develop an online Information Technology curriculum (http://www. teleeducation.nb.ca/it).

projects initiated by high school students to have significant impact on their future educational or career pursuits.

Collaboration efforts can be organized directly by the teachers and schools involved, or by taking advantage of one of the many ongoing projects already in existence. For example, Kidopedia (http://www.kidlib.org/kidopedia) is a Web site created in 1995 that allows students to contribute to a global encyclopedia. Students research a topic such as dinosaurs or asteroids and them submit an entry to the Kidopedia, adding to what has already been written by other students. The Global Lab (http://globallab.terc.edu) is a large-scale science project involving more than 100 schools around the world. Students at a participating school agree to collect and analyze common data about some aspect of their local environment (for example, a lake, river, atmosphere) and post their results on the Web site, so that everyone in the project can see the global trends.

Corporations and Government Agencies

Most large organizations make extensive use of networks, although more for information management purposes than anything having specifically to do with education. In fact, educational and training applications tend to be integrated with other applications in the form of help, performance support, or

Many technology companies, such as Microsoft Corporation (http://www.microsoft.com), are providing technical training online.

knowledge management systems (see Marquardt & Kearsley, 1999). Help systems are usually built into programs and provide explanations of how to use specific functions or accomplish certain tasks. Almost all commercial and proprietary software developed today includes some degree of online help. Performance support systems often include helps, but typically provide more capabilities in the form of demonstrations, frequently asked questions (FAQs), and resource databases with documentation, contacts, or problem-solving tools. Knowledge management systems attempt to accumulate and synthesize the collective experience of individuals in the organization by creating databases that cover all aspects of organizational activities and providing powerful tools to analyze them.

A number of companies have created electronic "corporate universities" based on the training programs they provide for their employees and customers (see http://www.corpu.com). Computer companies in particular (including Microsoft, Novell, IBM, and Sun) have been eager to offer online courses on hardware or software topics relevant to their products or services. U.S. government agencies, such as branches of the military, the Department of Agriculture, the Internal Revenue Service, and others, have moved their internal or public education efforts to the Web as well. However, much online training takes place via private intranets rather than the public Internet because of the confidentiality of the information provided on these systems. For this reason, it is difficult to examine or describe the extent of online education in the training world.

There are, however, a tremendous number of companies offering online courses aimed at the business marketplace. Many of these companies have targeted a specific training area such as financial skills (e.g., http://www.digitu.com), management/career development (e.g., http://www.athenaonline.com), safety/environmental topics (e.g., http://www.knowledgewire.com), or hospitality (e.g., http://www.HotelTraining.com). A general clearinghouse for online training courses is provided at http://www.alx.org.

Nonprofit Organizations

A wide assortment of nonprofit organizations play an important educational role in U.S. society, and many of them have developed an online presence. This group includes thousands of professional and trade associations that provide various educational activities for their members and the general public, including publications, conferences, and workshops (see Chapter 13 for a listing of those particularly relevant to teaching). In addition, large nationwide service organizations such as the Red Cross (http://www.redcross.org) and the AARP (http://www.aarp.org), as well as hundreds of smaller ones in every community, also serve educational functions.

One common goal of all such organizations is to find more cost-effective ways to reach their membership and the public. The Web provides a perfect solution, reducing their marketing and distribution costs while significantly increasing the potential audience. However, the Web only works if all members and the public have easy access to it—something that was not true by the end of the 20th century, but should be early in the 21st. In the meantime, these organizations are exploring the potential of the Web and determining how best to conduct their mission in an online environment.

The Home

Ultimately, online education could have its greatest impact in the home. Radio and television have done so, but with limited educational value. As the percentage of homes with computers gradually increases, it is likely that more and more educational activities will take place there. Adults will use computers for continuing education and job-related training; college and K–12 students will use them for schoolwork. Of course, a lot of online learning at home will be informal in nature, such as figuring out what's wrong with the cat, planning vacations, or shopping for a new car.

One area that will undoubtedly see a lot of development is online programs aimed at preschool education (Web sites for parents with young chil-

The Home School World site (http://www.home-school.com) is one of many online resources devoted to home schooling.

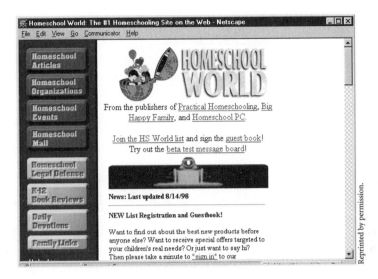

dren). A number of Web sites provide support for home schooling. We can also expect to see many sites catering to adult learning, either for leisure or new careers. This group includes all the nonprofit organizations mentioned previously, as well as those that specialize in home study programs (see http://www.dltc.org).

Public Spaces

Finally, one additional learning environment that electronic systems make possible is public spaces (Kearsley, 1994). Kiosks can be placed in shopping malls, libraries, airports, convention centers, hotel lobbies, cafeterias, hospital waiting areas, and other public locations. Although such systems typically provide general information such as location or services available, they can be used for more sophisticated purposes. For example, those located in medical facilities can provide patient or health policy information; systems at government service centers can provide explanations of application or claim procedures; even those in tourist information centers can provide historical background or access to community resources. Retailers are using public access systems in their stores to extend the range of merchandise available or to create a presence in locations where no store exists.

Historically, public access systems have been stand-alone devices relying on CD-ROM or magnetic disk for storage of data; however, it is becoming increasingly common for kiosk information to come from the Web. Direct

Travel information sites, such as this guide to Paris (http://www.paris.org), are excellent candidates for public access settings.

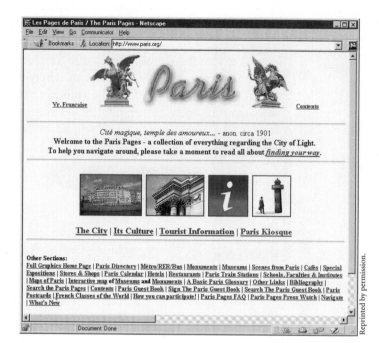

Reprinted by permission.

Web site access saves extra development work for the provider and means that the information is current (assuming the Web site is maintained). Kiosks in public areas provide a way to increase the accessibility of Web sites and make the information available in a setting where it is most needed or desirable (locations of initial public contact).

Margaret Riel: Learning Circles

Margaret Riel was one of the first researchers to focus on the development of global collaborative networks at the K–12 level. She led a project called "Learning Circles," which originally involved a partnership with AT&T and is now called I*LEARN. The key to this project was the formation of small groups that followed well-defined rules for online interaction. She was subsequently involved in the "Passport to Knowledge" project, which connects students to scientists and allows students to participate directly in scientific discovery.

She is currently the Associate Director of the Center for Collaborative Research in Education (CCRE) at the University of California, Irvine. Her home page is http://www.gse.uci.edu/mriel.html.

The kind of learning that occurs when people use public access systems is relatively casual and informal in nature. However, there is reason to believe that such learning is just as important as formal learning that occurs in the context of school. Public access systems allow us to provide much richer, more information-dense informal learning experiences than was previously possible in this kind of context. Public access systems are an example of the "anytime/anyplace" learning model that online networks and computer technology foster.

Conclusion

This chapter has provided a survey of the tremendous diversity of educational offerings that currently exist in online form within the United States and around the world (see also Berge & Collins, 1995, 1996; Khan, 1997). A wide assortment of different technologies are used to provide networked information within a given institution or organization, as well as to provide network access to individuals in their homes or public spaces. However, just because all of these opportunities for learning exist is no guarantee that they will be used effectively. Hence, the rest of the book examines in detail what we know about making online education work.

Key Ideas

- Although computer networks can be very complex, educators only need to understand a few details (how to get connected) to make use of them.
- Online education has developed quickly in higher education because the necessary infrastructure (equipment, software tools, technical support) exists.
- Applications of online education in K–12 schools emphasize access to resources and student collaboration.
- Corporate and government agencies are primarily concerned with information management and online documents, although some have developed performance support and knowledge management systems.
- Emerging areas for online education are nonprofit organizations, the home, and public spaces.

Questions for Further Reflection

1. What are the major problems with using networks in schools?
2. Are online classes more difficult to implement at the K–12 or higher education level?

3. Do you think that the emphasis on collaboration among schools will significantly change the nature of teaching or learning?
4. What are the pros and cons of online training in corporations?
5. How will online education change the nature of nonprofit organizations?
6. What kinds of problems do you foresee with online learning in the home?

3 Elements of Online Education

After completing this chapter, you should understand

- the different types of online applications and how they are used in learning and teaching activities
- the benefits and limitations of different online applications in the educational context

When we read electronic mail or send postings to an electronic bulletin board or make an airline reservation over a computer network, we are in cyberspace. In cyberspace, we can talk, exchange ideas, and assume personae of our own creation. We have the opportunity to build new kinds of communities, virtual communities, in which we participate with people from all over the world, people with whom we converse daily, people with whom we may have fairly intimate relationships but whom we may never physically meet. (Turkle, 1995, p. 10)

As we discovered in the preceding chapter, computers can be used in education in many ways. In this chapter, we discuss some of the basic elements of online education, beginning with email and progressing to more advanced topics like groupware and simulations. We will also talk about curriculum development and management tools.

Email

Email is the foundation for all forms of online learning and teaching. Indeed, it is quite possible to use nothing more than email in a course and still have a highly valuable learning experience. Email is also a very cost-effective application in terms of computing and network resources needed; it works with a minimum of equipment, software, and facilities. Furthermore, since Web-based email accounts are available at no cost from many sources (see http://www.emailaddresses.com), there is no need to buy email software.

Although email systems have become increasingly sophisticated over the years, they still provide the same basic functions (compose, send, reply, forward) as the early systems of the 1970s. However, most modern email systems (for example, Eudora, Netscape Mail, MS Outlook) cache messages and provide separate folders for different categories of mail (inbox, outbox, sent). The capability to cache messages means that mail can be composed and read offline, which minimizes connect time. Mail folders help you find and organize messages that have been sent, received, or are being composed.

The model for email use in a class is very simple: The instructor poses questions or problems (or they may be provided in a textbook or other curriculum materials), and students respond to them in their replies. Typically, there is a new assignment every week or two and a deadline when responses are due. The assignment may call for an extensive written response or a single answer in the form of a number, formula, drawing, or citation.

Eudora is a popular mail-reading program. This screen shows a list of all messages in the inbox (upper portion) and an actual message (lower portion). The message is an example of "junk" email. © 1999 Qualcomm Incorporated.

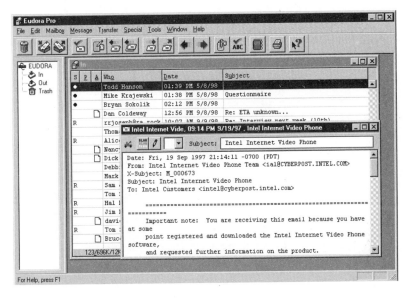

In the most cases, the response is sent as a private message to the instructor, who then provides feedback directly to the student via a reply. It is also possible to make this process more public by having students send copies of their responses to other students in the class or having instructors circulate feedback in the same way. Normally, however, the former pattern occurs in the context of group efforts, and the latter takes the form of a summary intended to wrap up an exercise or activity. When it is desirable to make class discussions public, a threaded discussion is usually more appropriate than email.

To ensure that everyone in the course receives all messages, an email distribution list will usually be used. A program called Listserv is commonly used in the Internet world for this function. A list is created with a unique name (for example, ed100-fall99), and email addresses are added to this list as "subscribers." When a message is sent to the list name and server address (for example, ed100-fall99@nebulus.com), all subscribers receive a copy of the message. Email distribution lists can be open, allowing anyone to subscribe, or closed, with subscribers limited to specific individuals (such as students registered in a course).

In addition to its formal use for assignments, email can be used informally by students to interact with instructors and fellow students. Whether students make use of this option or not (and most do), the fact that they can do so is an important psychological factor. Students know that if they want to ask the instructor a question or need help with a course-related problem, they can do so easily. Email significantly lowers the threshold for communication and makes everyone much more accessible than with traditional forms of education. Of course, this accessibility rests on the assumption that all participants (students, instructors, and administrators) read their email regularly—a fundamental condition for online education to work. Email use also involves some style considerations (for example, Angell & Heslop, 1994).

The main complications in using email are that systems are sometimes down, preventing messages from being delivered, and people change their email addresses. Most networks today will store a message that cannot be delivered and attempt to resend it at a later time—ultimately notifying the sender if it cannot be delivered successfully. When people change their email addresses, they can usually use a forwarding option that will automatically forward messages to the new address. Of course, this option only works if you maintain an account on the old system.

Threaded Discussions

After email, the second most commonly used capability for online education is a threaded discussion system, also called asynchronous conferencing, a forum, or a bulletin board. Although there are many different variations of these systems (for a survey, see http://www.thinkofit.com), they all work in the same fashion: topics and subtopics are created, and people post messages under any topic/subtopic desired. Messages include the sender's name, a subject title for the message, and the text of the message. To read messages, you select the topic/subtopic of interest and click on the messages available.

Conference systems can be set up in many different ways. New topics can be created by anyone, or only by the instructor. Only topics are displayed, with subtopics hidden, or all topics and subtopics are shown. Messages are posted directly, or messages must be previewed before being posted. Some systems identify new/unread messages, and some allow messages to be classified as explanations, disagreements, or follow-ups. Most systems allow people to edit or delete their own messages and allow the system administrator to delete or move all messages.

In the context of a course, each topic on the discussion board corresponds to a topic in the class. The instructor posts a question, issue, or problem as the discussion topic, and students post their responses as subtopics. Furthermore, students or the instructor may add comments to the responses posted by others. Thus, a discussion evolves over time as participants post their comments. Since everyone sees all the responses, this is a more public

Portion of a threaded
discussion that involved
an instructor interacting
with students in her class
and students at another
institution while attend-
ing a professional
meeting (ISPI).

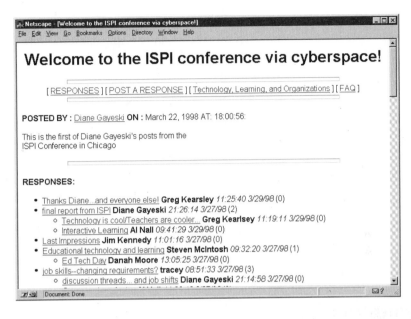

form of interaction than using email. And because all messages remain on the system, it is easy to review what everyone has said and follow the discussion.

This capability to retain all messages posted is actually one of the problems with a conferencing system; a well-used system will have hundreds of messages per topic, nested to different levels of subtopics, making it difficult to understand. Furthermore, participants are often careless about placing their messages in the appropriate topic or subtopic, which introduces considerable confusion into the discussion sequence. Unless the instructor or conference moderator expends considerable effort to keep the conference well-organized, it can turn into a chaotic jumble of messages. Part of this effort involves moving/removing messages posted in the wrong location and reminding participants to be more careful in their postings.

Real-time Conferencing

Real-time conferencing covers any form of online synchronous interaction. The simplest form of real-time conference is a chat session, in which participants exchange typed messages and everyone sees the messages as soon as they are sent. Each message is preceded by the name of the sender, so it is possible to identify who said what.

Because the interaction is in real time, it is spontaneous and dynamic. However, the discussion in a chat session is often difficult to follow because there are likely to be multiple conversations going on at the same time among different participants. Once a chat session has more than three or four participants, it is desirable to have a moderator who controls when people "speak." Participants indicate that they want to make a comment, and the moderator tells people when it's their turn. It is also the job of the moderator to keep people focused on a topic and balance the degree of participation by individuals.

When real-time conferencing is used as part of a course, the instructor usually defines the topic of discussion beforehand and moderates the chat session (or designates someone else to serve in that role). Alternatively, students can use chat sessions to work on joint projects or just to socialize without any involvement of an instructor. Most chat systems provide a save feature that allows the entire session to be saved as a file, which makes it possible to review the discussion later.

MUDs/MOOs

MUDs (multi-user domains) and MOOs (MUDs object-oriented) are an interesting category of real-time conferences used in some education settings. MUDs/MOOs allow many people to share a virtual world, usually set up as "rooms" containing objects that can be viewed or manipulated. People can interact with others by sending chat messages as well as performing simulated

Athena University uses a MOO for its Virtual Education Environment (http://www.athena.edu).

actions (such as standing/sitting, waving arms, running). The original MUDs were designed as "dungeon and dragon" games in which people would hunt for treasures. MOOs are a later development of MUDs that employ object-oriented programming techniques and are easier to develop and extend (including incorporating multimedia components).

MUDs/MOOs have been used in various ways for education. It is possible to create a virtual school that has rooms corresponding to different classes or learning adventures. In fact, Athena University is set up this way. It is also possible to develop a MUD/MOO for a specific subject area (for example, the periodic table, geological periods, historical events, cell biology) in which rooms correspond to major concepts and contain elements relating to those concepts. MOOs have been used to construct virtual zoos, science labs, and playgrounds. The English department at the University of Florida encourages students to conduct their class discussion in MOOville, a MOO that is part of their Networked Writing Environment (http://www.ucet.ufl.edu/writing). MUSENET (http://www.musenet.org) is a science education network based on the use of MOOs and virtual environments. E-MOO is a site dedicated to the use of MUDs and MOOs in education (http://tecfa.unige.ch:4243).

Desktop Video

The most advanced forms of real-time conferencing are desktop video systems. A desktop video system is basically a chat system that uses video images instead of text messages. The video images (including audio) are captured by a small digital camera that is connected to the PC. These cameras are relatively inexpensive ($100–$500) and can be connected to any computer (including laptops). Using software that comes with the camera or is obtained separately, it is possible to connect to a server running a videoconferencing program—or make a direct link with another person, using an IP address, for a two-person video session (called a point-to-point connection).

The videoconferencing software on a server allows many people to link up and transfer video images via the Internet. How many people can be linked up at once depends on many factors—the primary one being the bandwidth (transmission capacity) of the connections involved. People who are connected to a network via a modem and dial-up line will have the slowest transmission times, whereas those who have dedicated connections via T1 or LANs will have the fastest. So, a video conference involving participants who dial in using modems will be quite limited in the number of video images that can be displayed simultaneously; a group of people who are using T1 lines will have much better luck. In addition to bandwidth, the particular hardware (PC and type of camera) used will make a difference as well.

CU-SeeMe (http://www.wpine.com) is one of the earliest and most popular desktop videoconferencing programs, originally developed at Cornell University and now a product of White Pine Software.

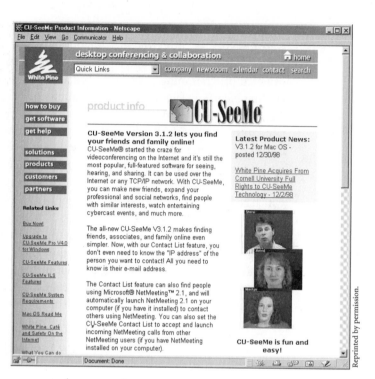

Reprinted by permission.

Machines with fast processors and large amounts of RAM will process images much faster than slower, less endowed PCs. Some cameras come with special video-processing circuit boards that speed up the processing dramatically.

Many desktop videoconferencing programs are available; CU-SeeMe is one of the oldest and most commonly used (see http://www.cuseeme.com). It can handle up to twelve simultaneous participants—which for practical purposes is ample. In any real-time conferencing situation (whether video or a simple chat session), it is very difficult to have a meaningful exchange of ideas with more than five or six people, even with an experienced moderator. This means classes need to be divided into small discussion groups for conferences—unless the conference is to be used basically as a broadcast, with one presenter at a time. In this approach, all other participants stay on "mute" (receiving but not transmitting) unless they have a question/comment and request permission to transmit.

Audiographics

A final category of real-time conferencing systems that needs to be mentioned is audiographics—systems that allow audio interaction and shared graphic images or applications. Participants in the conference can hear what the oth-

Microsoft Netmeeting is a widely used audio-graphics system (http://www.microsoft.com/netmeeting).

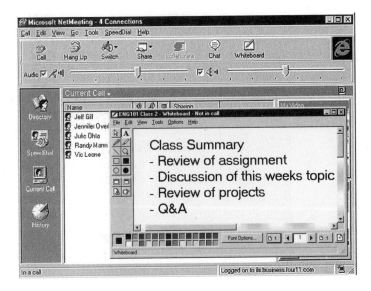

ers say and see the same graphic images or program screens. The graphic images are usually slides prepared with a slideshow program, although they can be drawn in real time on the screen by any of the participants (hence these systems are often called shared whiteboards). Alternatively, an application program running on one participant's system can be seen by all participants and, in most cases, controlled by anyone participating.

Audiographics systems are ideal for teaching applications that involve a lot of visual or graphical information (artwork, schematics, formulas, scripted languages). They are also well suited for courses that involve software use, because programs can be demonstrated and run while everyone in the class watches or takes turns working with them. They also require much less bandwidth and machine capability than videoconferencing, so they are more feasible for most students and school settings.

MS Netmeeting is an example of a widely used audiographics system. Although it is not as powerful as some of the more specialized systems, it requires only a single connection; others require separate data and voice connections. It provides audio- or videoconferencing (video is point-to-point), shared applications, whiteboard, chat, and file transfer.

Groupware

A relatively new category of software is groupware programs, which are specifically designed to facilitate group interaction. The MUD/MOO systems mentioned earlier are a specialized case of groupware for shared worlds.

Sample screen from GroupSystems program from Ventana East Corporation (see http://www.ventana-east.com).

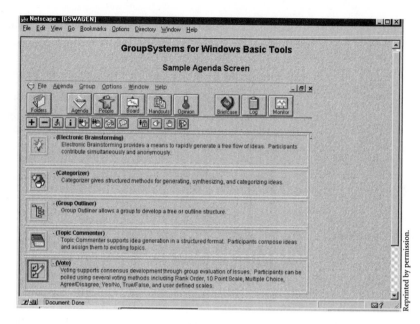

Lotus Notes, currently the most widely used groupware program, is popular in many organizations and university programs. For example, Athabasca University in Canada uses Lotus Notes as the basis for student interaction in its MBA program (see http://vital.athabascau.ca).

The primary focus of most groupware is on problem-solving and decision-making tasks, including such activities as brainstorming, poll taking, prioritization, and negotiation. Participants in a groupware session may all reside in the same building and participate via a LAN or be at remote locations using a wide area network (WAN). In a typical groupware setting, all participants are working on a common task, such as developing a budget, designing a new product, troubleshooting a problem, or selecting a course of action. A list of possibilities is generated based on input from each participant. Usually all input in a groupware session is anonymous, so participants are not constrained by their status or affiliations. Once a list is generated, all participants prioritize the items by rating/ranking them. The prioritized list is then shown to all, and discussion ensues (using a synchronous or asynchronous conferencing tool). This process can be repeated until a final decision is reached (or time/patience runs out).

Many variations are possible on this basic groupware model. For example, a small design team of three of four people will probably want to know exactly who says what—using some form of real-time conferencing (chat, audiographics, videoconferencing). Or there may be various levels of participants with different degrees of interaction (for example, contributors, editors, users). The software capabilities needed/available will vary across groupware settings.

Groupware is used mostly in business courses and management training at the present time (see Coleman, 1997; Lipnack & Stamps, 1997; Schrage, 1991). It is also very applicable to professional education (law, health care, engineering), which involves a lot of problem-solving and decision-making activities. However, as time goes on, and groupware becomes more general in nature, it is likely to be used in the full range of disciplines.

File Transfers

A mundane but nonetheless essential aspect of online interaction is file transfer—sending a file from one machine to another. In most cases, the file to be transferred is a word processing document, but it could be a spreadsheet, graphic, video clip, slideshow, or program. Since email is usually limited to relatively short text messages with no formatting, sending anything else requires a file transfer. File transfer is typically used by students to upload their assignments or download course materials.

The general purpose tool for transferring files is a utility program called FTP (File Transfer Program). To use an FTP program, you provide the server address for the machine you want to transfer the file to and then type in a

Using an FTP program to move files from one system to another.

valid user name and password. You then can select the directory and folder you want to upload to, or download a file from. To use FTP, you must have access to an account on the networked system unless there is a "public" account, called Anonymous FTP, that has no password and is used solely for file transfers. In any event, you must know the server address (for example, public.wadsworth.com), to make the connection.

Although use of an FTP program is a general solution for file transfers, simple documents (such as word processing files) can be handled directly by mail systems. Almost all mail systems allow file attachments to email messages, so it is not necessary to use a FTP program. This attachment feature allows students to turn in reports and other lengthy assignments as email messages to their instructor or teacher. Similarly, the instructor can send out course materials to students as attachments to email.

One of the technical complications of file transfer is differences in file formats. Everything other than a simple text file has a specific format that only certain application programs can read. For example, a document produced using MS Word 2000 will be saved in a format that only word processing programs compatible with MS Word 2000 can read. You will be able to transfer the file using FTP or as an email attachment, but the file will only be readable if it is opened with a compatible program. So, when transferring a file to another person, you need to be sure the recipient can read the format used. The safest way to ensure compatibility is to use an application program that resides on both systems. This is one of the reasons why course developers often specify that all students have the same set of software on their machines—to ensure compatibility for file transfers.

Application Software

Up to this point we have been discussing software exclusively concerned with networking. However, much (if not most) of the work in online education is done with routine application programs such as word processing, spreadsheets, graphics editors, and presentation software that are used to create instructional materials or do course assignments. Many courses use more specialized programs, such as math (for example, Mathematica, Maple, Matlab) or statistical tools (for example, SPSS, Statpak, MiniTab). In fact, almost every discipline has a variety of programs designed for certain teaching/learning activities. Some of these programs have been personally developed by instructors for use in their own courses.

The main consideration in using application programs in any course is how and when students will learn to use the software. Most instructors are reluctant to "waste" precious class time teaching the use of software, no matter how vital it is to completion of and success in the class. This is particularly true when the programs are standard applications such as word processing or spreadsheets. Teachers and schools have developed a number of strategies to handle this dilemma. One is to require completion of a prerequisite course teaching the relevant software prior to enrollment in classes that involve its use. Many colleges offer a "computer literacy" course that covers basic application programs. In other cases, computer courses are offered as independent study to be completed by students on their own schedule. Or the necessary training may be provided by supplemental/optional classes offered at the beginning of the course.

The issue of how well students can use application programs is very significant, because in many cases success in a course is directly affected by their computing proficiency. Furthermore, it is tied to an equity issue. Students who have access to machines and software at home are more likely to develop proficiency than those who have only limited access at school. So, students from financially disadvantaged homes who can't afford computers, software, and network connections continue to be at a learning disadvantage, perhaps a major one. For this reason, a number of government and private initiatives have been aimed at providing computer support for poor students.

Simulations

One of the well-established principles of learning is that performance improves with practice ("Practice makes perfect"). Yet in most cases, particularly school settings, students rarely get enough opportunity to practice the

Beverly Hunter: Computers as Tools

Beverly Hunter has been involved with computers in education for more than three decades and during that time has continually espoused the idea that computers are tools that should enhance learning and teaching. In 1983 she published *My Students Use Computers*, which outlined this perspective in detail. She has worked at a number of educational R&D centers, including HumRRO, TERC, and BBN, as well as serving as a program manager at NSF.

Most of her attention in the past decade has been on school networking (for example, http://www.ed.gov/Technology/Futures/hunter.html). She is currently at Boston College (http://www.learning.bc.edu).

skills or knowledge they learn. It is very difficult to design meaningful practice activities. However, computer simulations can change this situation significantly.

There are many different types of simulation, but all have the same fundamental structure. Simulations are based on a model of a specific system—mechanical, electronic, chemical, industrial, biological, or social. The student is presented with a system state that provides a number of choices; the choice made determines the next state of the system. In a science lab, simulations allow students to perform experiments or observe processes that are dangerous, expensive, or too time-consuming to do in actuality. Medical students can practice surgical procedures or diagnosis on simulated patients. Students in business schools can practice their marketing and financial skills with simulations of companies or industries. In the workplace, simulations allow people to practice operating or maintaining equipment ranging from telephone switching systems to aircraft. Even more interesting are simulations of human behavior that allow employees to improve their management, sales, leadership, or customer service skills.

Not only do simulations provide effective learning opportunities, but they can also be fun—when put in the form of simulation games. Finding a way to make learning more enjoyable is a primary concern when the learners are children and/or the home setting is involved (this is why MUDs appeared in the first place). A good example are the simulation games developed by Maxis Corporation (SimCity, SimLife, SimAnt, and so on), which began as

The ICONS project at the University of Maryland (http://www.bsos.umd.edu/icons) is an example of simulation applied to the international communications domain.

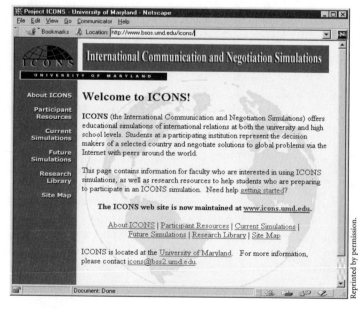

entertainment but have become widely used for educational purposes (see http://www.maxis.com).

Simulations usually involve a lot of graphics and multimedia components, which are used to depict events or elements of the simulated system. For example, simulations of equipment will depict control panels or switches that can be operated by touching the screen or using the mouse. Medical or biological simulations require graphics or animations to depict physiological processes (for example, the online frog dissection at http://curry.edschool. virginia.edu/go/frog). A sales/management simulation might use pictures or video clips to show people in work contexts (for example, http://www. smginc.com). Because simulations are so media intensive, they tend to be expensive and time-consuming to develop, which is one reason why their availability and use are limited. Furthermore, simulations are usually very interactive and require a lot of computing resources—systems with fast processors, ample memory, and lots of network bandwidth.

For more details about instructional simulation, see Gibbons and Fairweather (1998), Schank (1997), or Towne (1995).

Curriculum Development and Management

So far we have discussed online applications for direct instructional use. A large collection of programs is also available to develop and manage online instruction.

Course environments like WebCT (http://www. webct.com) provide a variety of course management functions.

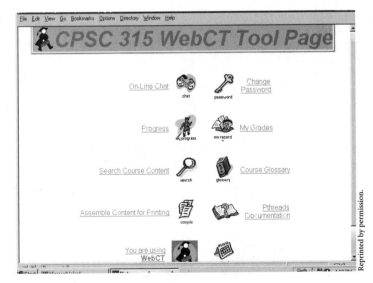

Many authoring tools are available for the creation of Web pages and sites (for example, FrontPage, Web-in-a-Box). Such tools make it relatively easy to assemble different kinds of information into a Web page and put it in HTML format (the formatting language used by the Web). Creation of multimedia involves the use of specialized programs for graphics, video, or audio editing. A program such as Macromedia Director might be used to produce an animation sequence for a tutorial or simulation. However, a large percentage of curriculum materials (course outlines, syllabuses, study guides, lecture notes) are created using standard application programs such as word processing or slideshow programs.

There are also quite a few Web-based course tools that integrate many of the applications discussed in this chapter (email, threaded discussions, real-time conferencing) into one package. Use of such systems makes it easier for students, instructors, and course developers because all applications work together from a common interface. Some popular examples are Topclass, BlackBoard, FirstClass, WebCT, and Learning Space. Such systems usually provide student grade book functions that make it easy for instructors to keep track of grades.

Comparisons and discussions of Web-based learning systems are provided at http://www.ctt.bc.ca/landonline/choices.html and http://cleo.murdoch.edu.au/asu/edtech/webtools/compare.html.

Finally, some institutions and organizations have developed their own course development or delivery tools that address certain instructional or administrative issues. For example, the University of Arizona has developed POLIS (Protocols for Online Learning and Instructional System), a Web cre-

POLIS is a Web development tool developed at the University of Arizona that facilitates the use of different instructional dialogues (see http://polis.arizona.edu).

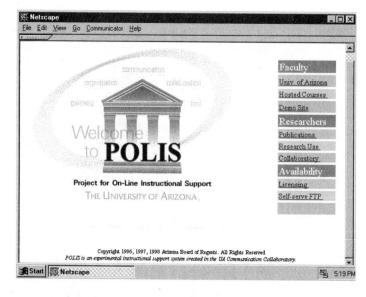

ation tool that provides templates for different types of student learning activities (for example, one-minute essay, recitation, argumentation, debate). A tool such as POLIS provides additional course design ideas for faculty (Jackson, 1997).

Conclusion

After reading this chapter, it should be clear that a variety of different forms of online education can be used alone or in combination for specific teaching/learning applications. Each one has its relative merits. For example, threaded discussions allow for reflective thought and deliberation on a topic, whereas real-time conferences have spontaneity and excitement. Simulations provide a structured learning environment, whereas MUDs/MOOs are quite unstructured. Email is a good method for assignments that involve short responses, but file uploading is needed for long documents or non-text files. For further discussion about how these applications are used in different educational settings, see Kaye (1992), Eastmond (1995), or Waggonner (1992).

In a subsequent chapter, we will examine the issues associated with using these various types of online applications for teaching and learning. But first, we will examine the research basis for online education.

Key Ideas

- Email is the most basic element of online education, providing interaction among students, teachers, and staff.
- Discussion forums allow for asynchronous group interaction.
- Real-time conferencing permits synchronous group interaction via chat sessions, MUDs/MOOs, desktop video, or audiographics.
- Groupware facilitates online group interaction, especially sharing of ideas.
- File transfer permits the uploading and downloading of documents.
- Application software provides tools for general and specialized course work.
- Simulations allow for online practice of skills.
- Curriculum development tools make it easier to create and manage online courses.
- An online course/program will involve a mix of these elements.

Questions for Further Reflection

1. One issue that often concerns people about online interaction is privacy. Under what circumstances should you expect remarks you make online

to be private? When is okay for them to be public? Does everyone feel the same way about this?

2. How does interacting with other people online compare to interaction in person? What about if you add audio- or videoconferencing capability? What aspects of in-person interaction cannot be duplicated with online interaction (if any)?

3. Online interaction is sometimes considered to be more socially "neutral" because it can hide physical characteristics (for example, race, gender, age, disabilities). Do you agree? Is this a good thing?

4. One of the ongoing issues associated with instructional simulation is the extent to which it needs to resemble the actual system being simulated in order to be completely effective. What is your opinion on this issue?

5. Some teachers and faculty oppose the use of applications and tool software in their classes because they believe it distracts students from the subject matter. How do you feel about this issue?

4 Research about Online Education

After completing this chapter, you should understand

- the different types of research studies about online education that have been conducted

- the typical evaluation results for online courses

- the impact of online education on school systems

In the beginning, human learning was limited to what could be accumulated in a single human brain in one lifetime. The invention of spoken language, then written language, then printing, and later, electronic communication media, expanded the human ability to accumulate and share knowledge among people and across generations. But all these innovations simply expanded the storage of information outside of the human head; the basic processes of thinking, deciding, and learning still were mainly confined within the skull. Technology is now extending the learning process outside the human brain and into the environment. Tomorrow's technology is quickly transforming the role of learning not only in human labor but in the economy as a whole. (Perelman, 1992, p. 51)

In this chapter, we probe the research basis for online education in studies of effectiveness, outcomes, and processes. But this research goes well beyond individual learning, because online education is an element of widespread social and economic change brought about by technology. We need to understand not only how the use of computer networks affects the way we learn, but also how we interact at work and home. Technology is pervasive, and so are its effects on education.

Impact on Student Achievement

The starting point for most studies of educational technology is an analysis of student achievement relative to traditional classes. In most cases, a course that has previously been taught in a classroom is now offered in online form, or perhaps both versions are offered simultaneously. If the course content, instructor, and student population are all the same, in theory any differences should be attributable to the different form of delivery. Alas, this isn't quite true, because it is likely that a course will be taught differently online than in a classroom (a topic we shall discuss at length in Chapter 6). However, as a practical matter, it is useful to know what impact an online version will have on student outcomes, using the conventional course as a base for comparison.

One of the most comprehensive studies of online courses was conducted by Starr Roxanne Hiltz and her colleagues at the New Jersey Institute of Technology with the EIES system developed there (see Hiltz, 1994). These studies involved undergraduate courses in sociology, English composition, management, computer science, and statistics. Evaluation measures included pre- and posttest course questionnaires completed by students, comparison

The U.S. Department of Education (http://www.ed.gov) is an important source of information about research in online education.

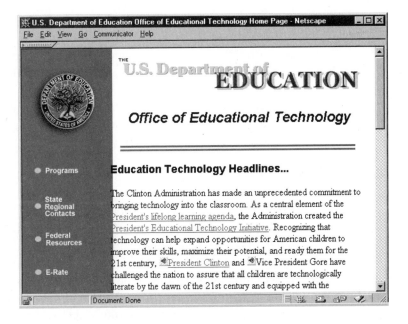

of test scores or course grades, direct observation of online activities, interviews with students, and faculty reports.

The Hiltz findings include the following:

- Mastery of course material was equal or superior to that of conventional classes.
- Students reported improved access to professors and educational experiences.
- Student participation in courses increased.
- Students reported higher satisfaction with courses.
- Students' ability to synthesize information and deal with complex issues/ideas improved.
- Level of interest in the subject matter of courses increased.

Although these findings were true of most courses, they were not true of all courses, depending upon the instructor and students. Hiltz concludes:

Results are superior in the Virtual Classroom for well-motivated and well-prepared students who have adequate access to the necessary equipment and who take advantage of the opportunities provided for increased interaction with their professor and with other students, and for active participation in the course. . . . Whether or not the Virtual Class-room mode is "better" also depends crucially on the extent to which the instructor is able to build and sustain a cooperative, collaborative learning group; it takes new types of skills to teach this new way. (p. 196)

In other words, online learning may work better for some students and instructors than others, as a function of their learning or teaching skills.

Evaluation of Web-based Courses

With the proliferation of Web-based courses at all levels of education, many evaluation studies have been conducted. These evaluations tend to look at different factors, depending on the interests of the instructor or course developers. Here are some examples at the college/university level.

Taming the Electronic Frontier (see http://www.virtualschool.edu/98a) was an introductory course in telecommunications developed by Brad Cox at George Mason University. The course evolved from a traditional on-campus course to a fully online version over a period of years as an exploration in the development of a distributed learning community (Cox, 1996). The course incorporated a number of different evaluation methods, including weekly assignments, exams, peer assessment, and a final evaluation survey. Grading was done on a mastery basis—that is, students could resubmit their work before the deadline until they got a "perfect" score. Students reported that they found the course challenging and highly motivating.

As part of the BIO project (Biology Instructional Outreach) at Iowa State University (http://project.bio.iastate.edu), Ingebritsen and Flickinger (1998) conducted an in-depth evaluation of one course, Zoology 155. A comparison of an online section of the course with a traditionally taught on-campus section indicated that the retention rates and final grades were similar, as were student attitudes toward science. However, students in the online section covered all the lecture material, whereas students in the on-campus section skipped 18 to 24 percent of their lectures. A separate study analyzed relationships between student achievement and learning styles/strategies in the online courses. It found that neither learning styles nor strategies affected achievement; that is, use of any learning style or strategy correlated positively with achievement.

At the University of Oregon, physics and astronomy courses have been offered in online form for a number of years (see http://zebu.oregon.edu). Bothun and Kevan (1996) have reported some of the results from the initial courses: improved student attention and engagement, higher exam scores,

Other useful sources of research about technology-based projects are the regional educational laboratories (see http://www.nwrel.org).

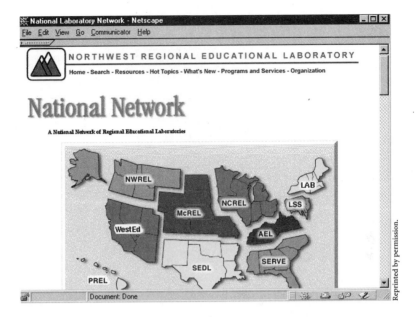

and better organized lectures and courses. They also report that some students were alienated by online courses because of the lack of in-person contact with instructors and other students. One interesting outcome was that attendance at optional on-campus lectures increased in the introductory courses, but decreased in the advanced courses. This suggests that students may need less in-person contact as they become more familiar with the subject matter and/or develop their self-study skills.

The library system of the University of Utah developed an online course called Internet Navigator to provide basic Internet skills to undergraduates. This was a credit course offered at most campuses, with librarians serving as local precepts (tutors). An evaluation study conducted by Lombardo (1996) indicated that students were very satisfied with the course (giving it an average rating of 4.11 out of 5), and almost half the students (49%) reported that they preferred to take an online course rather than an on-campus version. However, there was a serious problem with students' completing the course; only half the students finished (171 of 343). High dropout rates have been mentioned as a problem in a number of studies.

At the University of Illinois, the Sloan Center for Asynchronous Learning Environments (SCALE) has implemented a number of Web-based courses, using a variety of different course authoring and delivery tools (see http://w3.scae.uiuc.edu/oakley). The preliminary results indicate that students in the Web-based courses show improved retention, fewer dropouts, and more

Many high-tech companies actively fund research projects in educational technology. One major project is the Apple Computer ACOT program (http://www. apple.com/education/ k12/leadership/acot).

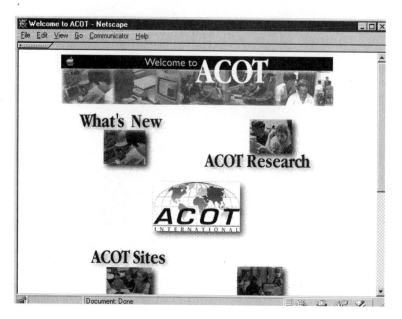

communication with faculty and other students. Students rated their online learning experiences very favorably, and faculty were highly satisfied with the outcomes of Web-based courses.

To summarize, course evaluation studies such as these typically find that students do at least as well in online courses as in traditional classes. Students consistently show higher levels of involvement in online courses, likely due to the increased interaction with their instructors and fellow students via email and conferencing. Some students do prefer traditional classes, and this preference may result in poorer performance if they are required to take an online course. It seems, however, that most students like online courses.

School-level Impact

Although student achievement and class interaction are important levels of analysis, it is also important to assess the effects of online education at the institutional or system level. Because online education is a major innovation that involves substantial changes in teaching methods and how learning is delivered, its overall impact on a school system or institution should be examined.

The Co-Nect project is a long-term effort to implement technology in school systems around the country (see http://www.co-nect.com). Some results of the project have included:

The Co-Nect project (http://co-nect.com) focuses on the impact of technology on school reform.

- A Co-Nect school in Worcester, Massachusetts, has seen steady improvements in all subject areas (fourth and eighth grades) on state assessment tests (MEAP). The gain from 1994 to 1999 was as high as 23 percent.
- Four Co-Nect middle schools in Dade County, Florida, showed significant gains on statewide writing assessments in their first year.
- An elementary school in Memphis, Tennessee, saw scores on the statewide fourth-grade writing assessment increase from 11 percent proficiency in 1994 to 39 percent proficiency in 1995.
- Many Co-Nect schools in urban areas report fewer student behavior and disciplinary problems.
- Teachers at Co-Nect schools find that students are assuming more responsibility and ownership of their schoolwork.
- Parents of students at Co-Nect schools are more involved in school activities and supportive of teacher/student learning efforts.

Many efforts to implement technology in schools (such as the Co-Nect project) are part of educational reform or school restructuring initiatives. Because technology represents only one of many innovations being attempted, it is difficult to attribute changes that result solely to the technology aspects. However, some school systems have made technology the primary element of their reform/restructuring endeavors, and this makes it easier to focus on the specific impact of online learning.

ERIC (Educational Resources Information Center) provides access to the research literature on educational technology (http://ericir.syr.edu).

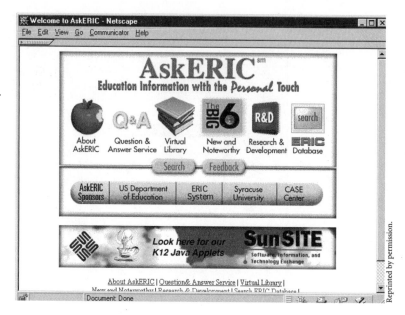

A good example is the Technology and Educational Reform project conducted for the Office of Technology, U.S. Department of Education, by SRI (Means et al., 1995). This study examined in detail the impact of technology (mostly, but not exclusively, online learning) in nine schools across the United States. The schools participating in the study varied considerably, from inner-city or rural schools with large proportions of "at risk" students to "model" or magnet schools with highly selected students.

The results were as varied as the types of schools and students involved. In some cases, improvements were observed in standardized test scores, although teachers and administrations tended to de-emphasize this outcome because they felt that such tests do not accurately reflect the changes that technology creates. Instead, they reported that technology increased the attention and study skills of students, helped them learn to assess their own abilities and those of others, improved self-esteem and motivation, and encouraged creativity. At one school, a survey indicated that the majority of students felt they had improved their problem-solving, writing, and reading skills, as well as their ability to work with other students. Finally, at some schools, technology was credited with improved attendance and reduced dropout rates.

Much work on the school-level impact of technology has focused in the changes that occur to school cultures. For example, Sherry (1997) reports on the Boulder Valley Internet project and the changes that occurred over a five-year period. Innovation and technology expertise were diffused through the

Many private foundations, such as the Benton Foundation (http://www.benton.org), pursue action research projects related to education and telecommunications.

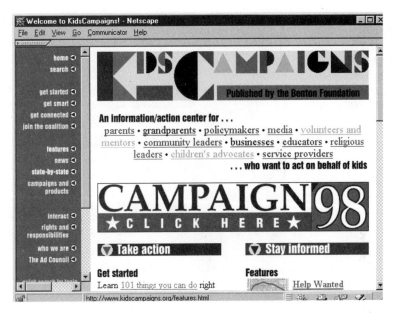

school system by teachers training other teachers, both formally and informally. Student use of technology shaped teaching activities. Moreinis (1996) describes the results of the Living Schoolbook project, which involved the introduction of computer networks at two New York City schools. The considerable restructuring of facilities and time schedules required to accommodate technology caused much turmoil. Persistence by teachers and students was needed to bring about changes that eventually resulted in successful computer use.

In summary, there is no doubt that online learning can have a significant impact at the school or school system level. However, the nature of the impact will depend on the particular circumstances of the schools involved, including student demographics, local/regional politics, and community goals/priorities. Furthermore, online education will necessitate significant changes to school cultures. We will address these considerations in more detail in later chapters.

The Nature of Class Interaction

One of the interesting questions about online classes is how computer use changes student and instructor interaction. Of course, the answer to this question depends on the exact nature of the class—which online capabilities are used—as well as the role of the instructor. Other factors that may affect

The National Science
Foundation (http://
www.nsf.gov) is a major
funding source for
research projects
involving technology in
science and mathematics
education.

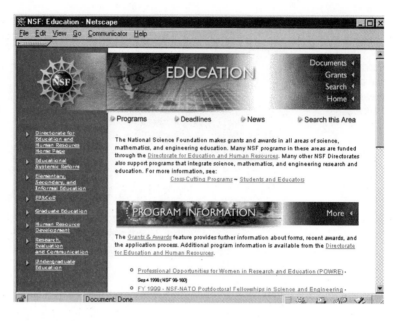

the nature of interaction are the discipline or subject domain, the level of
learning, and student backgrounds.

An online course can change the social context of a class, including the
amount of control exhibited by students and teachers. Ruberg, Taylor, and
Moore (1996) conducted a study in which they examined a collaborative peer
review activity in online courses for a freshman writing class and a plant science lab. Students had to read an article online, rate the article, then share
their views about the article in a synchronous conference session. The results
of the study showed that the peer review activity produced a high level of student participation, although the students who were the most frequent participants in the traditional classroom setting also tended to be the most frequent
online participants. The authors conclude: "Student dominance in the online
discussion was exhibited in several ways: (a) in overall volume the students
outnumbered the teacher, and student comments dominated the discourse in
quantity; (b) in some interchanges students took on more active roles of
regulating the discussion by reacting to comments by their peers with agree-
ment, evaluative comments, and follow-up questions and/or comments to
peer responses" (p. 86).

Hartman et al. (1995) examined the patterns of student interaction in a
freshman writing course at Carnegie Mellon University (CMU). The goal of
the course was for students to help each other become better writers. Two
sections of the course used online tools in the class, whereas two sections did

The NASA Classroom of the Future project is an R&D center for space science education located at Wheeling Jesuit University (http://www.cotf.edu).

not. The online tools included Comments, a program that allows easy annotation of a document, and Talk, a chat program that provides each participant in a conference with a separate message window. Their results indicated that use of the online tools increased total student–teacher interaction, but not total student–student interaction, relative to the conventional classes. They also found that the less able students communicated more with teachers and classmates electronically than the more able students and concluded: "The availability of electronic communication, in a sense, allowed a more equitable distribution of attention, especially from the more experienced teacher" (p. 71).

Collaboration is a common aspect of online courses, but it is difficult to assess student learning in this context. Students complete assignments or projects in small groups, and usually all share the same grade for the work. However, this grading approach does not identify the relative contributions of each student toward the success of the project. An alternative method is to ask students to document their contribution to the project and then assign separate grades to each student. Another way to grade projects is to have students create journals or portfolios of their work, and use these materials as the basis for evaluation of each student. This problem is not unique to online learning, but it does become more of an issue because of the tendency for students to collaborate.

Collaboration among students will be affected by their backgrounds and sociocultural factors. The COVIS (Collaborative Visualization) project of the Learning Sciences program at Northwestern University (http://www.covis.nwu.edu) is an attempt to improve science learning through the use of networks, with special attention to the development of tools for scientific visualization and distributed learning. Early results from this project indicate significant differences between urban and suburban schools in the use of computer networks: Urban schools value access to information, whereas suburban schools are primarily interested in learning improvement (Edelson, Pea, & Gomez, 1996). Furthermore, students from a lower socioeconomic background are less able to take advantage of open-ended research projects and need more structured activities. However, involvement in online projects creates engagement among all students.

Virtual Conferences

A virtual conference represents a larger scale of online interaction. Conferences are the primary means for continuing education among professionals. They provide an opportunity to hear about new developments and ideas, learn new techniques, and try out new products. They also provide social and recreational events to enjoy with colleagues and friends. However, attending conferences is time-consuming and expensive, which deters many doing so as often as they would like.

The virtual conference can provide most of the intellectual and social benefits of an actual meeting without the travel and financial complications. It can be offered as a supplement to an actual conference, occurring before, during, or after. All conference materials, including the presentations and conference papers, are provided on a Web site. Discussions between the presenters and participants are conducted as online discussions or chat sessions, or privately via email. Although most virtual conferences are conducted asynchronously using a threaded discussion, it is possible to hold them in real time along with the actual session. In this case, the presenter must have a computer at the podium to respond to online participants, and the screen needs to be projected for the on-site audience to see. The presentation can be distributed to remote participants using streaming audio or video (these are sometimes called "Webcasts").

Anderson (1996) describes the ICDE 95 online conference that involved 550 participants from 36 countries. The conference was divided into six sessions of a week duration, each using a different structure: debate, dialogue, brainstorming, nominal technique, open house, and panel discussion. All discussion was carried out via email using a Listserv, and one of the sessions also used a MOO. A total of 250 messages were logged, with an average of 14.6 messages per day over a three-week period (some sessions were concurrent). The conference was evaluated by means of a survey and by analysis of the session transcripts (see http://www.ualberta.ca/~tanderso/icde95). Evaluation results indicated that participants were highly positive about the experience, rating it as an excellent event. Participants did note that it took a lot of effort to participate and resulted in an overwhelming amount of information. Anderson concludes: "The virtual conference provides a means of eliminating the cost and unproductive time associated with travel and renting meeting space and accommodations. However, the virtual conference cannot create more time for busy practitioners. Professionals interested in lifelong learning must become skilled managers of their precious and limited amounts of time so as to maximize learning and social interaction" (p. 133).

Virtual conferences can also be events that substitute for actual meetings. One intriguing approach is to prerecord presentations by experts in digital audio/video format and then edit them together as a meeting. The presenters can interact with the audience in real time or in asynchronous discussion sessions at a later time. It is even possible to have panel sessions or debates by having each presenter respond to the same questions or issues and then assembling them together. This approach to virtual conferences has been used by the computer industry to create "summit" meetings of leading experts on important topics and issues. It is an excellent way to match up busy experts and executives without the need to take them away from their jobs or families.

Learning Communities

As mentioned in Chapter 1, the formation of learning communities is a characteristic of online education—an extension of the virtual communities that online interaction often engenders. The kind of student interaction discussed earlier in this chapter is the foundation for such learning communities, but it is only a part of them.

Learning communities extend beyond the timeframes of a particular course or conference and allow students to interact over an extended time period. Online degree programs that stretch over a number of years

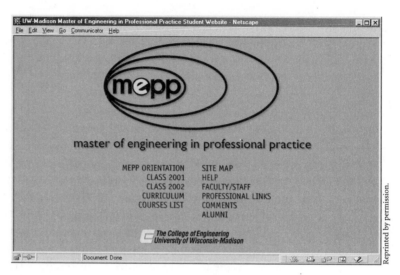

The Master of Engineering in Professional Practice (MEPP) program offered by the College of Engineering at the University of Wisconsin (http://mepp.cae.wisc.edu) is an example of a long-term online learning community.

represent a good environment in which to study the long-term effects of student interaction.

Kearsley, Lynch, and Wizer (1995) report some early data on the master's degree program in Educational Technology Leadership (ETL) at George Washington University (see http://www.gwu.edu/~etl). All courses in this program are online; there are no on-campus classes. Evaluation of graduates of the program indicates that they believe the technology skills acquired in the program has improved their work effectiveness. But equally important, participants in the program have developed a network of colleagues that they can draw on for advice and support in their job and career pursuits. Graduates of the program often serve as section leaders (tutors) in ETL courses and help establish links between past and new participants.

The interesting question in creating online learning communities is what features or facilities can be provided to facilitate long-term learning. Clearly, the availability of discussion areas that transcend particular courses is essential—along with user accounts that stay valid indefinitely. A directory of all participants is needed, one that can be modified by participants themselves as information changes. A newsletter that covers new developments in the field, to which anyone can easily contribute, can also be invaluable.

The development of online learning communities, with their effects on participants, is a new phenomenon in education. Historically, formal education has focused on the microscopic level of learning—that is, on particular classes or training events over a short period of time. But online education

Linda Harasim: Studying the Effects of Online Interaction

Professor Harasim has been active for more than a decade in researching educational applications of computer networking. She has designed, implemented, and evaluated networking applications in Canada, the United States, and Latin America. She is currently leader of the TeleLearning•Networks of Centres of Excellence project, which focuses primarily on the design and development of new pedagogies and network technologies to support collaborative learning, knowledge building, and lifelong learning. This project features more than 150 researchers from education, cognitive psychology, social science, computer science, and engineering science throughout Canada, collaborating online to address some of the major challenges Canada faces in becoming a learning society with a knowledge-based economy.

Her home page is http://fas.sfu.ca/telelearn/homepages/harasim/harasim.htm.

allows us to design learning experiences that are more macroscopic in nature, extending over many years. At the present time, there is much to be learned about this type of education, and we will need to devote much research attention to the subject.

For relevant background, see Bonk and King (1999), Garner and Gillingham (1996), or Palloff and Pratt (1999).

Conclusion

In this chapter, we have introduced some of the research associated with online learning and teaching. These studies have raised practical considerations that we will discuss further in subsequent chapters. They have also identified many questions and issues that need further examination in future research studies. Keep in mind that wide-scale adoption of online education is just beginning and almost all of the research needed in this area has yet to be defined or conducted.

It should be noted that online education is one form of learning at a distance and there is a legacy of research (and theory) about distance learning that applies (see Minoli, 1996; Moore & Kearsley, 1996; Porter, 1997). However, we have not taken the time here to explore these relationships.

Key Ideas

- Studies of student achievement in online courses suggest that most students learn effectively.
- Evaluations of Web-based courses indicate that these courses are just as effective as on-campus classes.
- The school-level impact of online learning depends on the characteristics of the students and the nature of the learning activities.
- Interaction in an online class creates a unique social context, much different from that of traditional classrooms.
- Virtual conferences seem to be a beneficial means of professional interaction.

Questions for Further Reflection

1. Do you think that participating in an online course results in a different type of learning compared to traditional classroom activities?
2. What role are individual differences likely to play in online education? How about socioeconomic or cultural differences?
3. Do you believe that online education works equally well for all subject matter and disciplines?
4. What characteristics of a school or school system make it more or less appropriate for online education?
5. How does online collaboration differ from in-person?
6. What are the factors that limit the success of a virtual conference?

5

Online Learning

After completing this chapter, you should understand

- how online learning compares to learning in a conventional class
- the characteristics of a successful online learner and an effective online learning environment
- how online learning applies to those with special needs

No matter how many times you visit the Basics Dome, its initial effect is literally stunning. It takes a while for the nervous system to begin processing; first you have to surrender to the overwhelming sensory bombardment that comes from every side. There are around us, forty learning consoles, at each of which is seated a child between the ages of three and seven, facing outward toward the learning displays. Each child sits at a keyboard, essentially less complex than that of an old fashioned typewriter, but fitted with a number of shifts so that almost every symbol known to human cultures can be reproduced. The child's learning display, about ten feet square, is reflected from the hologram conversion screen that runs all the way around the inner surface of the dome. The image appears to stand out from the screen in sometimes startling colors and dimensions. (Leonard, 1968, p. 147)

Learning online is much different than learning in a traditional classroom. In this chapter we will examine various aspects of online learning, including learning to learn, the social milieu, engagement theory, netiquette, computer literacy, special needs, and gender equity.

Learning to Learn

What is most different about online learning is that it usually provides the learner with a great deal of autonomy—the choice of when, where, and how to learn. We have described this autonomy earlier in the book as part of a student-centered approach to education. Learners are given a lot of freedom to pursue their own interests and methods of learning.

However, such autonomy brings with it responsibility. Learners must possess initiative and self-discipline to study and complete assignments. Students who lack these skills are likely to do poorly with online classes. Historically, online learning has been limited to graduate and professional courses in which students have good learning skills. But as online learning spreads across the entire spectrum of education and training, these skills are less widespread. As a consequence, online courses often experience high attrition and dropout rates.

A number of things can be done to address this issue. The first is to try to teach students how to be better learners. Many basic study skills can be taught, including time management, goal setting, and self-evaluation. Almost all of the techniques developed for traditional study apply equally well to online learning. Additional skills are also needed to do well as an online learner, including how to use software effectively, how to conduct online

Homework Central
(http://www.
homeworkcentral.com)
is one of many online
databases designed to
help students research
homework topics.

searches, and how to use communication capabilities such as email and discussion forums (for example, Campbell & Campbell, 1995; Reddick & King, 1996). Some online courses address these kinds of skills, but in many cases, students are expected to acquire them on their own—which is a problem if their basic learning skills are weak in the first place.

The Family Education
Network (http://
www.familyeducation.com)
provides support for
family learning—an
important context for
young children.

The Study Skills Help site developed by Carolyn Hopper (http://www.mtsu.edu/~studskl) provides help in learning skills.

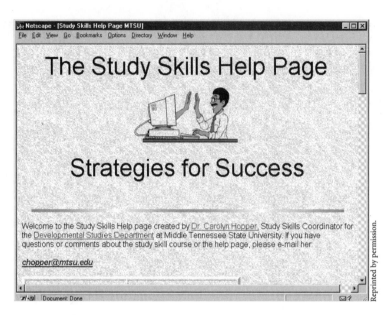

Another strategy for dealing with this issue is to try to increase the motivation level of the student. Students may have good learning skills but not be motivated to use them. We see this kind of situation often in K–12, where students are simply bored by the usual classroom activities. Online courses have the potential to challenge students and hence significantly increase their motivation to learn. The key is that students need to be engaged (see next section).

Basic writing and communication skills are also important for online learning, especially in the context of group interaction. In fact, this is one of the common reasons why students have difficulties with online learning. If students have trouble expressing their ideas in words, they will not be comfortable writing and responding to email messages, engaging in discussions, or producing reports. At the same time, online learning provides lots of practice in writing and communication, and teachers often report seeing improvement in these skills as a consequence of extensive online experience.

Being a successful online learner also means being good at learning to learn. The great difficulty for education in today's world is that information changes so quickly. In most disciplines and subject areas, there is a constant stream of new ideas, procedures, or methods. The way computers and networks operate is always changing, and so is the nature of online learning. Online learners must be adept at modifying the way they learn to match these changes.

The ESL Study Hall developed by Christine Meloni (http://gwis2.circ.gwu.edu/~gwvcusas) provides help in basic skills.

The Social Milieu

Online learning is as much a social activity as an individual one. Social skills are an important aspect of interacting via computer networks, especially when collaboration is involved. Alas, most people have little formal training in how to interact or work successfully with others; these skills are picked up incidentally through family or school life. To complicate matters further, the social milieu of online activities is quite different from in-person interaction and requires new skills and behaviors.

People will vary in the extent to which they participate in online discussions and conferences. Some will contribute frequently; others will read all the messages but rarely contribute (so-called "lurkers"). Level of participation is a function of several factors: (1) the assertiveness or shyness of individuals, (2) their interest and involvement in the subject matter, (3) their comfort level with the networking software being used, (4) convenience of access to the system, (5) their writing or speaking abilities, and (6) motivation/incentives to participate. Depending upon all these factors, a given individual may or may not contribute to an online activity.

Cultural considerations are also a major factor in online education (Cummins & Sayers, 1995; Warschauer, 1998). Many online classes involve students from different countries; indeed, one of the strengths of online education is the ease of conducting courses that have worldwide involvement. However, every culture has its own social customs that dictate the nature of

The All About Sex site (http://www.allaboutsex.org) is an example of informal learning outside the boundaries of traditional institutional course offerings.

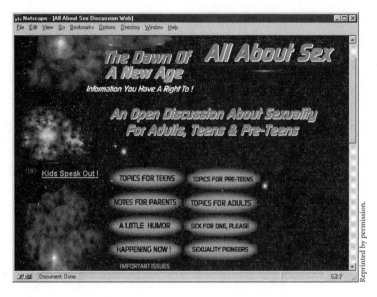

interaction with others (not to mention religious and political differences). Students and instructors must be sensitive to these differences and account for them when interacting with one another. One good way to deal with these issues is to encourage students to discuss them explicitly early in the course.

In general, asynchronous forms of interaction (email or threaded discussions) are less socially demanding than real-time conferences that require

The Oneida Indian Nation is an example of preserving a culture online (http://oneida-nation.net).

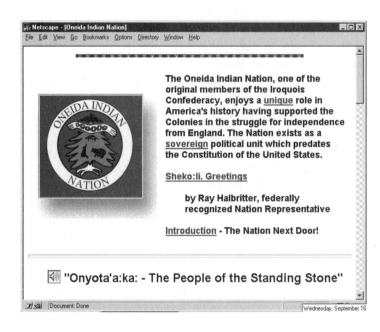

immediate and spontaneous responses. Asynchronous activities allow people to take as much time as they want to read and compose messages, which compensates for shyness, limited communication skills, or unfamiliarity with the software being used. They also allow people to reflect upon messages and their responses, resulting in more thoughtful discussions.

Finally, it should be noted that extended online interaction develops its own patterns of social behavior. This phenomenon has been well documented by Rheingold (1993), Rosenberg (1997), Strate, Jacobson, and Gibson (1996), Turkle (1995), Young (1998), and others. Certain conventions have emerged for online discussions (see the Netiquette section later in this chapter). An online class develops its own social milieu based on the nature of the online applications used and the way the instructor designs and conducts the course.

Study Web (http://www.studyweb.com) helps students find Web sites for specific subject areas of interest.

Engagement Theory

Over the years, many different theories and models of learning have been developed (see http://www.gwu.edu/~tip). Although many of these theories are relevant to online learning in some way, very few have been developed specifically in this context. An exception is engagement theory.

Engagement theory (Kearsley & Shneiderman, 1998) suggests that learners must be actively engaged in meaningful tasks for effective learning to occur. This means that they should be designing, planning, problem solving, evaluating, making decisions, or involved in discussions. Engagement theory

WebQuest (http://edweb.sdsu.edu/webquest/webquest.html) is an inquiry-oriented learning model that creates student engagement.

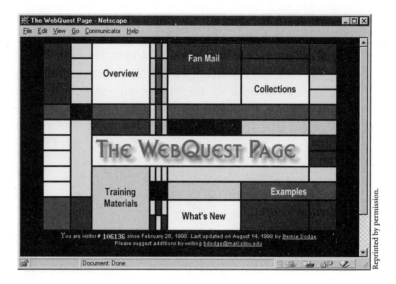

states that all learning ought to have three major characteristics: collaboration, problem-based, and authenticity. Collaboration means interaction among students, teachers, and subject-matter experts via email, discussion forums, and conferencing. Problem-based means that all student activities involve completing assignments or projects rather than taking tests or exams. Authenticity means that all course materials and activities are realistic and directly tied to the student's interests.

According to engagement theory, an online class should begin with students' getting to know one another, usually accomplished by having students post background statements in a discussion forum. An alternative approach might be an initial assignment requiring students to discuss their expectations and goals for the course. A second assignment might ask students to work in pairs or small groups to research a specific question. The next assignment might ask students (working in small groups) to analyze a case study or propose a design for a problem. A subsequent assignment might then be a major design or analysis project—a project that students would work on for the rest of class and present at the end. All of these activities would be conducted online, using the capabilities and tools discussed in the previous chapter.

Engagement theory is based on many major themes in learning theory. It espouses a constructivist philosophy, in which students are given the chance to create their own learning environment (Bruner, Piaget, and others). A constructivist framework is fundamental to the work of Seymour Papert, who was mentioned in Chapter 1. Constructivism is central to most areas of science and mathematics teaching (for example, Yager, 1991). Engagement theory also embraces the ideas of situated learning (for example, Brown, Collins, & Duguid, 1996; Lave & Wenger, 1990), which emphasize the importance of a community of practice. In addition, it is consistent with adult learning theories (for example, Cross, 1981; Knowles, 1978; Schon, 1990) that emphasize the experiential aspects of learning. Finally, it embraces the ideas of cooperative and team learning.

For many years, schools of business and medicine have emphasized a case-based or problem-based approach to learning. See, for example, the sites of the Harvard Business School (http://www.hbsp.harvard.edu/products/cases) and the School of Medicine at Ohio State University (http://www.med.ohio-state.edu/PBL). While these approaches to learning/teaching have been developed in the context of traditional classroom instruction, their emphasis on realistic and experiential learning is similar in nature to engagement theory. Indeed, it is likely that case and problem-based approaches will become more popular strategies in online courses since they can be implemented more effectively.

Netiquette

Interacting with others online requires some specific communications behaviors—conventions that have come to be called "netiquette" (Shea, 1994).

Here are some common "rules of the road" for the information highway:

1. Keep messages short. People don't like to read long email or forum messages. If you have a lot to say, break up your ideas into multiple postings.
2. Don't use CAPITAL LETTERS extensively in messages (especially not the dreaded all-caps message). Capitals are the online equivalent of shouting—something we don't normally do a lot of in polite conversation. Use them only when you want to really emphasize something.
3. When responding to an email message or conference posting, it's nice to begin by summarizing in your first sentence what you're responding to ("I don't agree with John D's comments about virtual sex . . .") so the context for the message is clear.
4. When you refer to a Web site, always give the URL so people can check it out themselves. It's nice to put the URL in executable form (include the http://) so the link can be selected directly.
5. Avoid sarcasm in messages because it is easily misinterpreted. Online messages don't carry the tone of voice and facial cues that indicate a remark is meant to be humorous, so it is likely to be taken as an earnest comment. If the message is in video format, this concern is diminished.

The Albion Netiquette site (http://www.albion.com/netiquette).

6. Be wary of "flaming"—getting involved in an online argument by making thoughtless or nasty remarks in a message. Because they are written and context-free, negative comments tend to be amplified, which means that minor insults or criticisms seem much harsher. You need to be careful when formulating online messages—it's not the same as in-person or telephone interaction.

Just as some people are excellent at in-person communication, some individuals become masters at online interaction. Of course, this involves more than simply understanding netiquette; it means that the computer network has become so transparent to them that they are able to focus completely on the interaction. Over time, we can expect many students to attain this state. However, there will always be some individuals who don't feel comfortable with online interaction. How we can accommodate these individuals is an important issue.

The Netiquette Guide, written by Arelene Rinaldi, is available in ten languages (http://www.fau.edu/netiquette.net/index.html).

Computer Literacy

One of the major concerns for most students (as well as their teachers and parents) is understanding computers well enough to use them effectively in their studies. Actually, this seems to a more serious problem for older stu-

Students need good online learning tools. The Yahooligans search page (http://www.yahooligans.com) makes it easier for kids to find information on the Web.

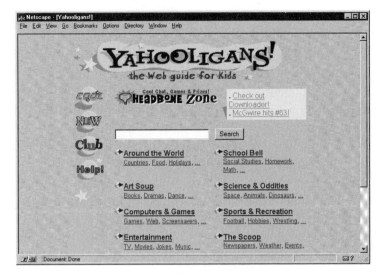

dents (college and adult learners) than young children, because the latter are growing up in a technology-rich world and seem to assimilate computer concepts quite easily.

All high school students today are expected to have a command of basic computer applications such as word processing, graphics editors, databases, and spreadsheets, as well as how to connect to the Internet, use email, and browse the Web. At the college level, students are often expected to master additional software programs for specific disciplines such as mathematics, statistics, or engineering. Knowing how to use a search engine (such as Yahoo, Altavista, or Lycos) is an essential skill for doing research on the Internet, whether at the K–12 or graduate level.

In the business world, computer literacy needs are even more demanding. Employees of corporations and government agencies must learn to use proprietary systems for customer billing, financial processing, inventory, manufacturing, and so on. In addition, employees must know how to read email, access product information and customer records, or produce reports. In some jobs, people spend their entire day working at a computer (for example, stockbrokers, air traffic controllers, travel agents, retail clerks, customer support representatives). Many countries have made improving the computer literacy of their population a national priority; Finland, for example, has developed a "Computer Driver's License" (see http://www.tieke.fi/tieke/ajokortti).

Clearly, the computer proficiency of students and employees determines their success in school and in the workplace. Given this fact, the question arises as to how much attention should be given to teaching computer skills. Most schools, colleges, and organizations now devote a significant amount of time to computer literacy in their courses and training efforts. However, most individuals still acquire most of their computer knowledge via self-learning. Consequently, a student's or employee's natural interest and desire to learn about computers is a very important factor in computer literacy and online education.

Special Needs

Certain groups of individuals have special needs and hence pose particular concerns for online education. These groups includes young children, senior citizens, and individuals with disabilities.

Young children have limited reading and writing abilities, and hence cannot usually use standard network programs or tools. Instead, they need software that is highly visual in nature or makes use of audio/video explanations. Specialized email and other application programs (such as word processing, graphics, and database) have been developed for children based on this approach. To the extent that online learning involves games and hands-on activities, it seems to work well with young children. Druin (1999) and Healy (1998) provide discussions of some of the issues associated with the use of computers by children.

Many children have learning disabilities such as attention deficit disorder, dyslexia, or speech problems. There are numerous support groups, treatment/training programs, information databases, companies, and consultants available online that focus on one or more of these disabilities. See, for example, the Learning Disability Association at http://www.ldanatl.org and the Council for Exceptional Children at http://www.cec.sped.org (the latter site also includes the ERIC Clearinghouse on Disabilities and Gifted Education). These online resources are very useful to teachers as well as the parents of students with disabilities.

Senior citizens may encounter a few user-interface limitations in terms of screen readability and typing capability because of vision or psychomotor impairments, but most systems and software today can readily compensate for these problems. For example, Web browsers allow the size of the type on the screen to increase until it is fairly large. Similarly, operating systems normally allow for a variety of different input devices, including mouse, joystick, or touch screen.

For those with more severe disabilities (such as autism, deafness, blindness, multiple sclerosis, or cerebral palsy), a wide range of assistive hardware and software is available (see http://www.trace.wisc.edu). This technology in-

Seniornet (http://www.seniornet.org) is an example of an online community focused on the interests of a specific group of learners: older adults.

cludes text-to-speech synthesizers and Braille printers for the blind, speech input devices for those with no physical mobility, and text captioning of audio elements for the deaf. Unfortunately, many school systems and employers are not aware of such technology or lack the expertise to install and maintain it. Consequently, parents, teachers, and individuals with disabilities often have to be very persistent (frequently to the point of taking legal action) to get schools and companies to provide assistive technology.

Project EASI (http://www.rit.edu/~easi) provides guidelines for development of online materials for individuals with disabilities.

The graphics and multimedia features of the Web present a problem for individuals with certain disabilities, but increasing attention is being paid to designing Web pages that minimize these problems (see Chapter 7). The irony of designing extended capabilities for special needs is that these capabilities are often helpful to all users. For example, the capability to enlarge text size in any program is handy when you want to show something on the screen to a large group—or you can't find your reading glasses. So, addressing special needs in the design of software and hardware ought to become routine, rather than something done as an afterthought.

For more background information about computers and disabilities, see Cook and Hussey (1995), Coombs and Cunningham (1997), Covington and Hannah (1996), or Lazzaro (1996).

Gender Equity

Another important social/cultural aspect of educational computing is the inequity between males and females in computer activities (Furger, 1998). Beginning in the early grades of school and continuing through college and employment, relatively few females are attracted to technology, making it a male-dominated environment. Girls are not encouraged to "play" with computers, nor to pursue computer-related studies or careers. Clearly, this gender gap is a problem for an information society in which half the population is disenfranchised.

The roots of this problem are in cultural norms, which are not easily changed. However, some educators have developed programs that specifically target girls and attempt to get them more interested and involved in

Norman Coombs: Adaptive Technology for Online Communication

Norm Coombs is a professor of history at Rochester Institute of Technology and a pioneer in online education. As a blind person, he makes extensive use of adaptive technology to teach. Interestingly, his interaction with deaf students in classes provided him with an initial understanding of how online interaction could provide new learning opportunities. He has been the chair of the EASI project and involved in many efforts concerned with access for individuals with disabilities. He was also named New York Professor of the Year in 1998.

To learn more about his background and work, see his home page at http://www.rit.edu/~nrcgsh.

technology. An example is the Cyber Sisters Club developed at Penn State Lehigh Valley by Judy Lichtman (see http://www.lv.psu.edu/jkl1/sisters), which provides a supportive environment for girls to explore computers. There has also been a proliferation of female-oriented online groups such as the Canadian Women's Business Network (http://www.cdnbizwomen.com) and the Russian Web girls (http://www.russianwebgirls.com). For an interesting analysis of women and cyberculture, see "Girls Need Modems" by Krista Scott (http://krista.tico.com/mrp.html).

In the long term, gender inequity is likely to disappear as women take more jobs in technology and hence provide role models for young girls. However, this progression could take many years in certain cultures (countries and organizations) and may not happen at all in societies dominated by religious fundamentalism. But then, such fundamentalist cultures are not likely to embrace online education anyway.

Conclusion

Being a successful online learner depends on a number of factors, including having the necessary learning-to-learn skills, adapting to the social milieu (including cultural obstacles), being engaged in the learning activity, following the rules of netiquette, and having a suitable interface. Most students at the postsecondary level or employees participating in training efforts can readily satisfy all of these conditions. For students at K–12 levels or individuals learning by themselves, it may be more difficult. How easy or difficult learning is for a given course depends in part on the instructor and the design of the online activities—considerations we look at in the next two chapters.

Key Ideas

- To do well in online classes, students need to have good study and communication skills, be highly motivated, and be capable of learning to learn.
- Online learning takes place in a social milieu that emphasizes interpersonal interaction and is sensitive to cultural considerations.
- Engagement theory provides a framework for online learning that is based upon collaboration, authentic content, and problem-based activities.
- Netiquette provides a set of conventions for online behavior that everyone should follow.
- Students and employees need certain basic computer skills to be successful online learners.
- Certain populations of learners, such as young children, older adults, and individuals with disabilities, have special needs in terms of computing.
- Efforts need to made to avoid gender bias in online education.

Questions for Further Reflection

1. Do you consider yourself a successful online learner? Why or why not?
2. What concerns do you have about the social aspects of online interaction?
3. Identify other learning theories or models that are relevant to engagement theory or online learning.
4. Can you think of any additional rules of netiquette?
5. What special needs seem to present the biggest problems for online learning?
6. Are some people likely to learn better online than from traditional means?

6

Online Teaching

After completing this chapter, you should understand

- how online teaching differs from traditional classroom instruction
- the qualities of an effective online teacher

The Information Marketplace will change the role of schools, universities, and the educational community. One of the more obvious effects will be the simultaneous expansion of the student market for schools and the school market for students. Why study at a local school, training center, or university, if you can attend at a distance, the best school for your particular interests? (Dertouzos, 1997, p. 187)

In the previous chapter, we discussed how learning online differs from learning in conventional educational settings. Similarly, teaching online is very different from traditional classroom practice. In a classroom, the teacher tries to impart information and get students enthused about the subject matter. But in an online class, the teacher's job is more like that of a coach or moderator than a presenter or performer. To the extent that the student is engaged in active learning, there is less need for extrinsic motivation from the instructor. And because information can come from databases or collaboration, the instructor doesn't have to be the content expert. Furthermore, online courses provide many opportunities for teachers to collaborate, and team teaching is becoming a common element of network-based courses.

Interactivity and Participation

The most important role of the instructor in online classes is to ensure a high degree of interactivity and participation. This means designing and conducting learning activities that result in engagement with the subject matter and with fellow students. As discussed in the previous chapter, course work should focus on assignments and projects that are relevant and realistic in nature. It should involve plenty of opportunities for input from the instructor and fellow students. This condition can be readily satisfied by having students post their work in a threaded discussion forum where everyone can see and comment on all responses. The use of an email distribution list serves the same purpose, although it does not allow for the cumulative discussion possible in a forum.

Even though the means for online interaction and participation are provided, students will still need encouragement to get involved. Such encouragement is especially needed for students who are new to online learning or professionals with busy work schedules. The most effective approach is to make participation a course requirement and a component of the grade. Each assignment can be graded on the overall quality of participation by the student. Interaction among students can be further increased through peer

The World Lecture Hall (http://www.utexas.edu/world/lecture/index.html) is a worldwide database of online courses at the college level.

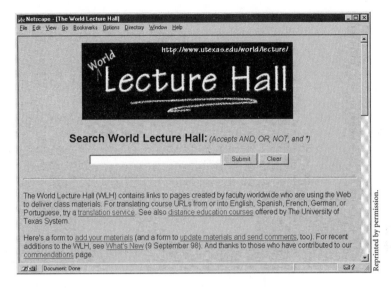

Reprinted by permission.

evaluation activities and team assignments. In a nongraded course or one with voluntary participants (such as an internal workshop), interactivity and participation will depend mainly on how useful and relevant the activities are to the students. To the extent that the assignments and discussions are personally interesting and worthwhile, students are likely to participate without any extrinsic motivation. Thus, use of the engagement model, which

The Awesome Library for Teachers developed by Jerry Adams (http://www.awesomelibrary.org) is one of many online curriculum databases available for K–12 teachers.

The Newspapers in Education site (http://www.dnie.com), a project of the Detroit News and Free Press newspapers, is an effort to extend publishing resources to the online world.

Reprinted by permission.

emphasizes meaningful and realistic course work, is even more critical in these settings.

Another factor that strongly affects the amount of student interaction and participation is the level of instructor involvement. If the instructor regularly posts messages in the discussion forum or provides comments to students via email, this input increases student involvement and participation in a course. A cardinal rule of good online teaching is that the instructor must participate a lot to get students to do likewise.

It should be noted that although participation and interaction are closely related, they are not the same thing. Participation refers to involvement and presence, without any response or feedback being involved. For example, many students may participate in a real-time conference, even though only a handful may actually have any interaction. Interaction means that some sort of dialogue is occurring between the student and the instructor, other students, or the content itself. Content dialogue means that the system responds to student input or choices—for example, responding to a question or search query. Simulations are highly interactive, because the state of the system changes instantly based upon student actions. Obviously, it is desirable to have both participation and interaction in online learning programs. Both can be achieved through the use of the various tools discussed in Chapter 3 in ways that are appropriate for the learning goals and objectives of the course (Levin et al., 1989).

Among the many associations and organizations concerned with online education is EDUCAUSE (http://www.educause.edu).

Reprinted by permission.

Feedback

A primary task of the teacher is to provide feedback. In online courses, teacher feedback will generally take the form of email messages about assignments or comments on assignments that students have submitted. The instructor will usually mark up the original file submitted by the student, then have the student download it to see the comments. Ideally, the instructor provides individual feedback to each student, as well as group feedback. Group feedback may take the form of messages posted in a discussion forum or conference summarizing/synthesizing the individual responses given on a topic or activity.

Peer evaluation can be an alternative or supplement to feedback from the instructor. Feedback from fellow students is often quite helpful because it comes from their perspective rather than an expert's. However, students normally need detailed guidance in evaluating one another's work, such as a checklist, a set of questions, or a list of criteria. It may also be necessary to remind students to be constructive in their comments; students tend to assume that evaluation needs to be negative. Asking students to review the basic principles of netiquette discussed in the previous chapter is also a good idea.

The timeliness of feedback is very important. Students are often anxious to know if their work is acceptable or correct (Crouch & Montecino, 1997). And from an instructional perspective, feedback is more valuable in correcting

The Training & Development Community Centre (http://tcm.com/trdev) is an example of a resource for those interested in the training world.

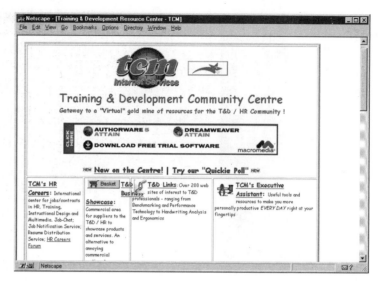

misunderstandings if it is received as soon as possible following the initial response. Even if the feedback is a simple acknowledgment that the work was received, it makes a big difference to students. Indeed, one of the most common complaints students have about online courses is that they did not get timely feedback (or any) on their assignments. Teachers should indicate the normal turnaround time for feedback on assignments (for example, within 48 hours) and ensure that they achieve this standard. The same rules on providing timely feedback should apply to peer evaluation activities as well.

Workload

One implication of making a course highly interactive and providing good feedback to students is that it creates a high workload for instructors (Brown, 1998). As a rule of thumb, the higher the level of interactivity and participation in a course, the more work is involved for the teacher. Organizing and moderating online activities takes a lot of time. If a class has thirty students in it and the instructor spends an average of twenty minutes per student evaluating their work and providing feedback each week, this amounts to ten hours per week for one class—a significantly higher workload than for most traditional classes. Keep in mind that this time estimate covers only student interaction; it does not include time spent preparing course materials, learning to use software, and troubleshooting problems.

Teachers Helping
Teachers site developed
by Scott Mandel (http://
www.pacificnet.net/
~mandel).

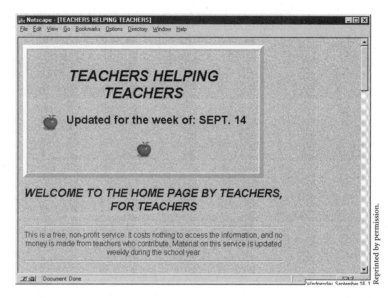

One way to reduce this workload is to rely more on peer evaluation activities, in which students evaluate one another. However, instructors still need to monitor peer evaluation activities and sometimes intervene. Another potential strategy is to rely primarily on group feedback messages rather than individual ones. Creation of a FAQ (frequently asked questions) file or page is a good method for handling commonly repeated questions (see Shaw, 1966).

The use of teaching assistants or aides is another strategy for reducing workload that is especially applicable for large classes. In general, an online class larger than thirty students is more than a single instructor can handle comfortably. When teaching assistants are used in online courses, however, they need to have online experience, preferably as students. They will likely need to be trained in the basic techniques of online teaching. Also, they need to supervised in terms of the quality of their work, either by the instructor or the course manager. Given all these considerations, the use of teaching assistants in online courses is not a simple solution to handling large courses, even though it appears to be an easy one.

The easiest way to provide feedback to students is through the use of multiple-choice or short answer tests. Indeed, most online testing tools provide for automatic scoring and generation of feedback messages to students immediately upon completion of the test. Although the immediacy of feedback is ideal, test scores and predefined feedback messages on these kinds of tests do not usually provide meaningful learning experiences. If the engagement model is being practiced, students are involved in projects or writing

OnlineClass (http://www.onlineclass.com) provides a database of online lessons and guidance for teachers about how to integrate them into classroom activities.

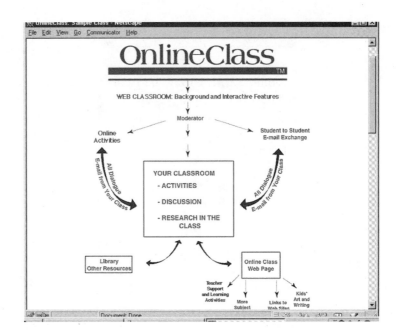

responses to assignments, and such testing is inappropriate. Although simple tests do make sense in some settings (such as solving math problems or mastering terminology), in most cases their use indicates a failure to design good learning activities.

Even though the workload for an online course may be high, it provides more flexibility than teaching a traditional class because teaching activities can be done where and when desired. This flexibility is one of the major incentives for faculty to teach online. So, the convenience of online education is important to both students and instructors.

Moderating and Facilitating

It has been mentioned previously in this chapter and earlier in the book that online teaching requires good moderating and facilitation skills (Berge, 1996; Paulsen, 1995). Moderating involves encouraging students to participate in discussion forums and conferences, ensuring that certain students don't dominate, keeping discussions focused on the topic at hand, bringing out multiple perspectives, and summarizing/synthesizing the highlights of discussions. Facilitation means providing information that will help students complete their assignments, suggesting ideas or strategies for them to pursue in their course work, and getting students to reflect on their responses and work.

These moderation and facilitation activities take place at various levels. At the beginning of a class, the instructor may discuss with students their specific expectations and goals for the course, given their background and previous online experience. When grading individual assignments, the instructor will be providing feedback appropriate to the capabilities and background of each student. In the context of a conference or discussion forum, the instructor will be trying to get all students to participate and to learn from one another. Similarly, in the context of group projects and collaborative activities, the instructor will be focused on getting students to work together and benefit from the team interaction.

Adopting the role of moderator or facilitator in online classes significantly changes the nature of a teacher's role and workload. It requires the teacher to pay more attention to the social dynamics and patterns of interaction in the class. It also requires the teacher to focus on the individual needs and progress of each student in order to facilitate their learning. There is much less emphasis on presenting information and more on helping students find information. Teaching a particular lesson or topic may take longer than in a traditional classroom because some students may take longer on their own to acquire the skills or knowledge desired.

One of the dilemmas that most instructors face when they begin to teach online is that they have little experience with moderating and facilitation techniques (unless perhaps their background is in elementary or special education, where these methods are commonly practiced). These skills need to be a key element of any training program designed to prepare instructors for online teaching. Teachers who have these skills already will have a big advantage in the online environment.

Effectiveness

A number of factors determine the effectiveness of online teaching. Among the most obvious is experience, including both a general familiarity with the nature and techniques of online teaching and mastery of the particular system and software used in a given course. For example, experienced online teachers will know how to use and manage a discussion forum for course work, but they must also be adept at using the particular forum software used in a course. Because course delivery tools and the network are continually changing, instructors will need to spend considerable time learning new software in advance of its use for classes.

Effective online teachers also need to understand and practice all of the techniques discussed in this chapter with respect to interaction, participation, feedback, facilitation, and moderating. These skills are usually developed

The Searle Center for
Teaching Excellence at
Northwestern University
(http://president.scfte.
nwu.edu) is one of many
teaching effectiveness
centers throughout the
United States.

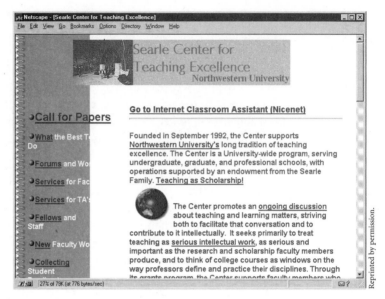

over time as a teacher gains more experience with online classes. However, they can be acquired more quickly if teachers have experience as students in online courses and hence understand what it's like to learn in an online environment. For this reason, it is highly desirable that training for online teaching be conducted via online courses.

Effective online teachers are most likely to be good teachers in general. Studies of teacher effectiveness show that good teachers are enthusiastic about teaching and about their subject area, are very concerned with helping students, are willing to try new teaching methods and ideas, and are interested in improving the quality of their teaching. These qualities predispose good teachers to be effective online instructors, but they do not guarantee that all good teachers will be effective online teachers. Some excellent teachers who enjoy classroom presentations and in-person contact with students do not find the online environment as rewarding or comfortable to teach in. And some good teachers do not have the interest or necessary skills to teach online. It is also possible that teachers who don't do well in the traditional classroom might do better with online classes, although this outcome seems less likely.

Tinker and Haavind (1996) have reported on the results of their Netseminar model, designed to prepare teachers in the Virtual High School Cooperative project for online teaching (see http://www.concord.org). A netseminar is an online training course that introduces teachers to the kinds of collaborative and constructivist learning approaches that they will use with their students. Tinker and Haavind observe that online teaching requires a cultural shift on the part of teachers, to value and capitalize on the collabora-

The @ONE project is a consortium of ten California community colleges that provides training, evaluation, and technology planning support for its members (http://one.fhda.edu).

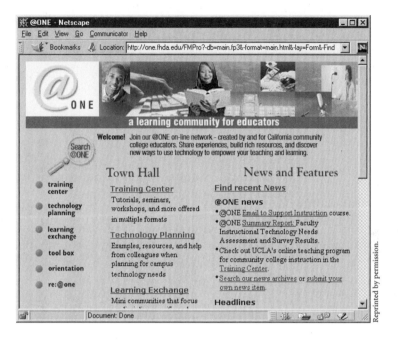

tive potential of networked activities as well as improve partnering in face-to-face school contexts between site coordinators and teachers. For example, although teachers could easily share ideas with one another, broadcasting information one-to-many and team-teaching a virtual course, the culture of creating a lesson plan alone is normative practice. In other words, becoming a successful online teacher involves a lengthy change process in terms of teaching methods.

Faculty Collaboration

Just as online courses offer many opportunities for student interaction, they also provide many possibilities for collaboration among teachers. Although teachers usually like to collaborate, they often find it difficult to do so in a conventional classroom setting. However, an online class makes collaboration easier.

One common model of online collaboration is to have "guest" participants for a specific class or course topic. For example, an expert in a certain topic might be asked to join a real-time conference or a discussion forum and respond to student questions or comments. Most people are willing to do this for free because it takes relatively little time and does not involve any more inconvenience than signing on to the computer. If the interaction is more extensive (stretching over a period of days or weeks), the guest is likely to be paid an honorarium or a consulting fee.

In preparing the course, the primary instructor identifies potential guests (usually from their publications or conference presentations) and then contacts them via email to see if they are interested and available to participate. If they agree, a specific time frame for their participation is worked out, and they are asked to provide any relevant background materials in electronic form (Web documents). Both guests and students usually find these experiences very worthwhile and stimulating. Not only does it introduce students to differing perspectives on the subject matter, but it also establishes connections to other institutions and organizations.

Another form of online collaboration is when two or more faculty from different institutions jointly develop and offer a course through both their institutions. Students from each of the participating institutions can take the course for credit, and it counts as part of the teaching load for each faculty member. This kind of team teaching is more difficult to organize than the guest participation model because the course must be approved administratively by the relevant departments and committees at each institution (often no small task). However, this approach has many advantages. It allows resources of multiple institutions to be pooled in the development and delivery of a course, and students get the benefit of interacting with one another across institutions.

Finally, there are many opportunities for informal collaboration via email, conferences, and discussion forums. Faculty frequently contact au-

The Access Excellence Web site (http://www. accessexcellence.org) is a nice example of business–school–government partnerships. It was created by Genentech as a resource for high school biology teachers and will be part of the National Health Museum Web site.

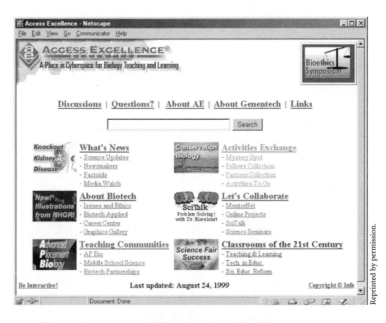

thors or researchers about their work and make use of these interactions in their teaching activities. Developers of products are usually eager to talk to users and discuss problems or ideas related to their software. Teachers often refer their students to conferences and discussions that are relevant to the class being taught, and sometimes students bring them to the attention of their instructors and fellow students. Indeed, in the network environment, it's difficult to not collaborate.

Student Evaluation

An aspect of online teaching that often generates considerable concern for teachers is evaluation of student performance. They worry that they will not be able to assess student understanding or participation properly. Ironically, student evaluation can be done far more effectively online than in a traditional classroom setting.

All student responses can be recorded (including actual key presses and screen selections), providing a wealth of data to analyze. The pattern and history of a student's course participation can be taken into consideration when assessing performance. If learning activities in a course involve frequent assignments in the form of written responses that are posted as messages in discussion forums, conferences, or via email, all of these responses can be aggregated into a student portfolio (either by the teacher or by the

The data recording functions available in the course delivery tool are an important element of student evaluation. This example shows the gradebook function of the CourseInfo BlackBoard system (http://www.blackboard.com).

student). The results of assignments and exams can be kept in a database and included in the student's record. One of the most useful functions that course delivery systems provide is a student record function that make it easy for teachers to create and maintain such records.

Although the engagement model discussed in the previous chapter favors student assignments in the form of problems, projects, case studies, and the like, it is certainly possible to conduct any kind of test or quiz desired. For example, tests with time limitations can be done in the context of real-time conferences in which all students must begin and end at the same time. Alternatively, the questions can be posted at a certain time and students required to submit their answers by a certain deadline (perhaps 24 hours later). A number of companies provide online testing services for schools (for example, http:// www.webtester.com), and many online test tools are available (see http:// sunil.umd.edu/documents/assess.html). Major aptitude tests such as the SAT are also becoming available for administration online (for example, http:// www.kaplan.com). The Educational Testing Service (http://www.ets.org) is a good site for researching issues concerning online testing.

One of the issues frequently raised about online student evaluation is cheating. How do you know that the responses on the screen come from the actual student, not some substitute? Generally this is not a significant problem in full semester courses because faculty get to know the characteristics of students and should be able to detect differences in individual behavior. In cases where major exams are involved (such as certification or achievement tests), students may be required to take exams in a specific location where a proctor checks identification (for example, http://www.sylvan.prometric.com). Finally, videoconferencing can be used to make visual identification of the student. Indeed, as desktop video becomes more commonplace, this issue may become a very minor one.

Betty Collis: A World Perspective on TeleLearning

Although she began her career as a mathematics teacher in the United States, Betty Collis has been a professor for many years in the Faculty of Educational Sciences and Technology at the University of Twente in the Netherlands. She has been involved in numerous projects to assess the effectiveness of computers in European school systems as well as research studies of online learning. She has written many publications, including the comprehensive textbook *TeleLearning in the Digital World*.

To learn more about her work, see http://www.to.utwente.nl/user/ism/collis/home.htm.

When peer evaluation is used in courses, the guidelines that students are to use in evaluating each other's work must be clearly defined. Checklists that list each of the points to be assessed, along with the grade/rating for each, are very useful. Although students may generate the grades, the teacher should be responsible for recording them and should reserve the right to make adjustments if necessary.

Conclusion

This chapter has tried to outline the characteristics of online teaching and explain how it differs from teaching in a traditional classroom. One of the big questions for all educational institutions is how best to train existing and new instructors for online teaching. One clear answer is that teachers must acquire some experience as online learners in order to properly understand how to teach online. So, there is an urgent need to put teacher training courses in online form. As subsequent generations of students who have taken courses online become teachers, this need will diminish. However, the nature of online teaching is shaped by the particular network and software technologies available, and this technology changes constantly. So, teacher training for online education will have to be ongoing, even for those with considerable experience.

Many of the considerations discussed in this chapter with respect to teaching roles and workload have major policy and organizational implications. We will address these issues in the chapters that follow. For further discussion of online teaching, see Harasim et al. (1995), Leshin (1996), Steen et al. (1995), or Williams (1995).

Key Ideas

- One of the main tasks of an online instructor is to ensure a high level of student interaction and participation.
- Instructors must provide meaningful and timely feedback to students in online courses.
- A primary role of the online instructor is to moderate and facilitate student discussions.
- The teaching workload of an online course is usually heavier, and strategies are needed to deal with this added demand.
- The effectiveness of online instructors is a function of their experience with online teaching, mastery of the online environment, and overall teaching skills.
- Faculty can collaborate in online teaching in a variety of different ways.
- Student evaluation in online courses can be very comprehensive, based on the recording of student activities or automated testing.

Questions for Further Reflection

1. Are all instructors capable of being good online teachers?
2. What are the advantages and disadvantages of online teaching?
3. Is online teaching more difficult than traditional teaching?
4. What is the relationship between good online teaching and effective learning?
5. How does online teaching affect the relationships among teachers?
6. What new possibilities does online evaluation offer?

7

Design and Development of Online Courses

After completing this chapter, you should understand

- the design considerations in creating an online course

- the nature of online curriculum materials and the authoring tools available to help create them

The greatest challenge for designers of future systems consists in providing users with the fullest possible set of advantages with respect to the computer's potential for human communications, with a minimum of knowledge needed to involve the capabilities. (Hiltz & Turoff, 1993, p. 327)

This chapter discusses some of the considerations in creating online courses, including development methodology, form and function, course documentation, integrating on-campus activities, and the authoring process. Although we will talk about the course creation process in relatively analytical terms, it is actually a very creative endeavor, not always rational and orderly in nature. However, certain rules reliably produce better results, and we will focus on those rather than dwell on the mystical aspects.

Development Methodology

Over the years, methods for the development of instruction have been explored and refined. The most widely adopted methodology is the Instructional Systems Development (ISD) model. Although the ISD model has many variations, it basically suggests that an instructional development project be divided into five major stages: analysis, design, production, implementation, and evaluation (see Dick & Carey, 1990; Hannum & Hansen, 1989; O'Neil, 1979). Associated with each of these stages are certain techniques, such as task analysis, definition of objectives, media selection, and formative evaluation, that involve increasingly detailed specification of the instruction to be delivered. Indeed, the ISD model is an attempt to use an engineering approach to the creation of instruction based on top-down planning and well-defined procedures.

Although the ISD model was not specifically developed for the creation of online courses, it has been used for this purpose, especially in large organizations. Its primary virtue is an emphasis on writing design specifications, requiring details to be thought out before any development work begins (thus preventing much wasted effort). At the same time, the ISD model encourages a somewhat linear development strategy that is often too lengthy and expensive for real-world projects and school settings.

An alternative development methodology is minimalism, which originates from the computer and technical publications world rather than training (see Carroll, 1990, 1998). Minimalism is based on the iterative design approach commonly used in the computer field and involves the development of prototypes. A prototype is developed, tested, and refined—eventually pro-

Big Dog's ISD page is an online guide to ISD developed by Don Clark (http://www.nwlink.com/~donclark/hrd/sat.html).

viding the basis for the working program. The primary strength of the iterative model is that faster progress can be made in development. However, this progress is often made at the expense of well-thought-out designs, which ultimately results in a weak product.

Minimalism suggests some design principles for instruction that are quite different from those usually associated with ISD. For example, it recommends identifying goal states for a learning task, without necessarily outlining all the intermediate steps. With ISD, all steps needed to accomplish a task are outlined. Minimalism emphasizes the importance of including error information (what to do when something goes wrong), which is not part of the ISD model. Minimalism also proposes that learning tasks should be closely integrated with the system being learned, whereas ISD does not address the context of learning.

ISD and minimalism represent two well-established methodologies for the development of instruction (neither of which is specific to the creation of online courses). A developer may choose to follow one of these models, or neither. However, such models provide procedures that have been used many times and increase the chances of producing successful instruction. For this reason, it is recommended that novice developers try to follow an established model such as ISD or minimalism until they are sure they have a better approach of their own.

A number of style guides are available for the design of Web sites, including one developed by the Center for Advanced Instructional Media at Yale University (http://info.med.yale.edu/caim/manual/contents.html).

Yale Style Manual-Table of Contents - Netscape

File Edit View Go Communicator Help

Yale C/AIM Web Style Guide

Patrick J. Lynch
Yale Center for Advanced
Instructional Media

Sarah Horton
Dartmouth Curricular
Computing
Dartmouth Didactic Web

Search this site:

Search

Detailed search page

Philosophy

Introduction
Purpose of the site
Design strategies

Interface Design

Introduction
Basic interface design for the Web
Information access issues
Navigation
Links & navigation

Site Design

Introduction
Site structure
Site elements I
Site elements II
Intranet design factors
Site Covers

Document: Done

Reprinted by permission.

Form and Function

Development methodologies such as ISD and minimalism provide a series of guidelines based upon instructional considerations (for example, Briggs, Gustafson, & Tillman, 1991; Leshin, Pollock, & Reigeluth, 1992). However, the creation of online courses involves at least two other categories of design principles: usability (function) and aesthetics (form).

Usability refers to how easy a program is to use. Human factors (also called ergonomics), the discipline concerned with usability, has a whole sub-field devoted to the usability of computer systems (for example, Galitz, 1997; Hix & Hartson, 1995; Shneiderman, 1998). Usability principles include rules such as the following: (1) Always have the system acknowledge user input. (2) Allow the user, not the system, to establish the pace. (3) Make it easy for the user to recover from errors (an undo function). (4) Provide multiple input methods, such as pointing and typing. (5) Always provide default selections. Principles such as these are based on human factors research that has looked at how people learn best and why they make mistakes when using computers (see http://www.useit.com).

Usability principles have to do primarily with interactivity and the processing of user actions. However, software design has a whole other side: screen design. Although screen design is mostly a matter of aesthetics, some usability aspects are involved here too. Principles such as the following have to do with the legibility and layout of screens: (1) Use an appropriate number

A number of U.S. research labs study computer usability, among them the Human–Computer Interaction Laboratory at the University of Maryland (http://www.cs.umd.edu/projects/hcil).

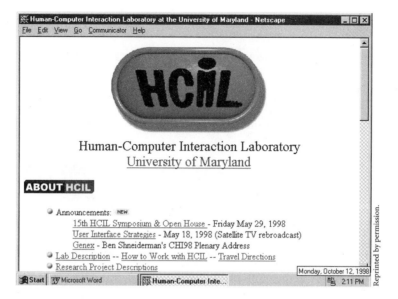

and selection of type fonts. (2) Use attentional devices sparingly. (3) Avoid screen overcrowding. (4) Use titles and headings to organize information. (5) Use appropriate color combinations for text and backgrounds.

One further design consideration is the creation of programs and Web sites that are usable by individuals with disabilities. The primary concern is to ensure that all input and output functions allow for alternative processing modes, such as movement of the cursor via the keyboard instead of the mouse, enlargement of screen displays, text-to-speech conversion, and so on. The developer should check that a program works with built-in system functions such as the Microsoft Windows Accessibility utilities and major categories of assistive technology. For Web sites and pages, certain rules must be followed with respect to HTML (such as use of the "ALT Text" field for all graphics). The Center for Applied Special Technology (CAST) provides Web design guidelines for universal access, along with its "Bobby" checking and validation system (see http://www.cast.org). Another useful site for Web design guidelines and discussion about universal access is http://www.webable.com.

The aesthetics of screen displays has to do with how information is presented and organized. Considerations include the use of graphics and colors, font (typestyle) choices, and text arrangements. Aesthetic principles are concerned with getting the attention of users, motivating them to learn, and creating excitement about the program. When a course is used in a self-study setting, it needs to sustain the student's interest over a long time period. Aesthetic considerations also extend to the use of sound, animation, and other multimedia elements (see Boyle & Boyle, 1996; Druin & Solomon, 1996; Howlett, 1995).

Good design involves achieving a balance between usability and aesthetics. You want a program or Web site that is easy to use, but is also visually interesting and highly motivating. The difficulty of achieving this combination is one reason why there are relatively few outstanding programs and Web sites.

Most large colleges and universities have an instructional technology center that supports faculty development efforts. An example is the Academic Technologies for Learning center at the University of Alberta (http://www. alt.ualberta.ca).

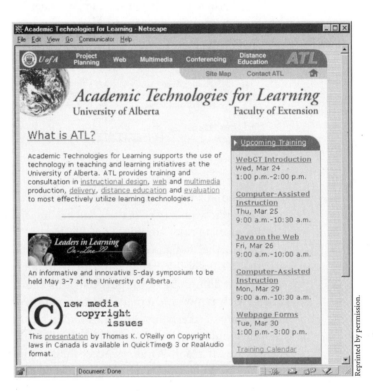

The Team Approach

One of the major differences between developing online course materials and traditional print materials (such as textbooks and lecture notes) is the need for a team approach. It is difficult for a single individual to have the range of skills and time required to develop an online course. To begin with, the design of an online course should start with a careful analysis of the student population to determine not only what they need/want to learn but the nature of their computing capabilities and learning environment. Assumptions are often made about computer skills or accessibility that are not valid and limit the success of an online course. These kinds of needs assessment data are normally collected by instructional designers as a routine part of their design activities (but rarely by subject-matter experts or teachers when creating courses on their own).

Even though faculty are usually subject-matter experts and familiar with how the content should be taught, they typically have little experience developing course materials for online learning. An instructional designer or performance technologist can work with faculty members to develop the various course components in suitable form. Most universities and organizations have instructional technology groups that provide this kind of support, or outside consultants may be hired.

Most online courses will require (or benefit from) graphics in the form of illustrations, diagrams, icons, and backgrounds. Incorporating these elements involves graphic design skills and knowledge of graphics software. In addition, if the course involves any audio or video elements, a person with a background in and understanding of multimedia production will be needed. Likewise, the creation of animations or simulations will require special programming help.

Although most of the software tools used in an online course (as described in Chapter 3) can be purchased or acquired in ready-to-use form, they still need to be implemented on a particular server, and this installation often involves some debugging effort. So, technical support is required either from within the institution or from an outside vendor. In order for instructors to set up the online learning environment the way they want it, they must work closely with technical support personnel.

The bottom line is that development of an online course normally involves the joint efforts of numerous specialists, including instructional designers, graphics or multimedia designers, and systems analysts/programmers. Although it is possible for individual teachers to create entire courses on their own, this requires a tremendous time investment and willingness to learn about many aspects of instructional design and software implementation. Most faculty would prefer to focus on the content aspects of a course and leave the rest to others.

Course Documents

A number of documents can be used to organize and structure a course. The most common is a syllabus that includes course goals and objectives, discussion of prerequisites, an outline of class activities and schedule, a description of course grading and evaluation methods, a list of texts or readings, and a bibliography. It should also tell students where to get help if they need it

An example of a lesson plan from the Lesson Plan Exchange of the Engaging Science site (http://www. engagingscience.org/lpe/ lpe.htm).

(content, technical, or counseling). The syllabus is the blueprint for the course and gives students the essential information they need to know. Syllabuses for online courses are no different from those for traditional classes, except that they may include links to relevant resources.

A second important document is the lesson plan, which describes how a teacher plans to conduct a class. The lesson plan is similar in nature to a syllabus, including a description of goals and objectives, prerequisites, class activities, and evaluation methods. However, lesson plans are usually more detailed in terms of class activities; they identify specific actions to be performed by the teacher, including preparation steps. Lesson plans often must show that the objectives or learning outcomes of classes adhere to those established by state curriculum guidelines.

A third important course document is a study guide. The study guide is intended to help students understand the course content better; it usually provides additional explanations and examples of the subject matter, as well as practice problems/exercises (with answers). Study guides are usually provided in distance learning courses to integrate the other course materials and activities. An online study guide can provide links to resources for further study. It may also contain lectures or presentations in the form of slide shows or audio/video segments.

The three documents just described (syllabus, lesson plan, and study guide) are routine components of an instructional program and not unique

One of the issues that becomes important when integrating on-campus and online activities is electronic classrooms (see http://classrooms.com).

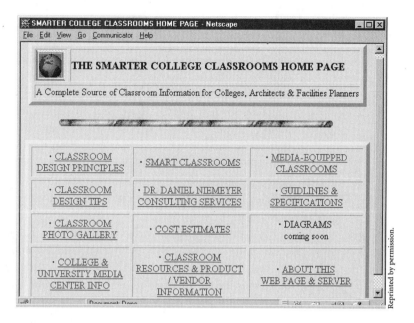

THE SMARTER COLLEGE CLASSROOMS HOME PAGE

A Complete Source of Classroom Information for Colleges, Architects & Facilities Planners

· CLASSROOM DESIGN PRINCIPLES

· SMART CLASSROOMS

· MEDIA-EQUIPPED CLASSROOMS

· CLASSROOM DESIGN TIPS

· DR. DANIEL NIEMEYER CONSULTING SERVICES

· GUIDLINES & SPECIFICATIONS

· CLASSROOM PHOTO GALLERY

· COST ESTIMATES

· DIAGRAMS coming soon

· COLLEGE & UNIVERSITY MEDIA CENTER INFO

· CLASSROOM RESOURCES & PRODUCT / VENDOR INFORMATION

· ABOUT THIS WEB PAGE & SERVER

Reprinted by permission.

to online courses. In recent years, efforts have been made to develop standards for Internet-based instructional materials to facilitate sharing of courses across institutions. One such effort is the Instructional Management Systems (IMS) initiative, a partnership of many corporations and government agencies hosted by EduCause (see http://www.imsproject.org). The main idea behind the IMS standard is to develop a common set of course descriptors (called metadata) to be used by all organizations to document their online courses. Typical descriptors include topics/subject matter, course objectives, availability, course author(s), prerequisites, course length, hardware/software requirements, and evaluation data available. By adhering to the same standard, it is possible to create databases of information about courses that are meaningful and can be easily searched—paving the way for sharing of courses across institutions.

The creation of some form of specification for online courses (whether in IMS format or not) is a good idea for large-scale development efforts. Such specifications facilitate coordination among the development team as well as maintenance (revisions) of courses over their lifetime. Specifications can also help to ensure that all course materials have a common visual identity and contain the same essential elements. Thus, they can play an important role in quality control (see Chapter 9).

Integrating Online and On-campus Activities

As a general rule, most online courses and programs will involve some on-campus activities. These activities may include orientation sessions, hands-on labs, examinations, lectures, or discussion groups. Many instructors and students do not feel comfortable going through an entire course without some form of in-person contact, even if this contact is only social in nature. Furthermore, some courses involve hands-on or interpersonal activities (for example, surgery, engine repair, drama) that require physical facilities or interaction. It is also beneficial for students to receive training on software tools in a campus lab setting with an instructor present to provide immediate assistance.

A typical arrangement is for students to attend an on-campus session once at the beginning of the semester, another at a midpoint, and a third at the end of the course (which may involve taking an exam). Many graduate programs have only one on-campus session at the beginning of each term (two or three per year) or one weeklong annual session in the summer. The frequency of on-campus sessions will be dictated by the nature of the curriculum (need for hands-on or in-person interaction) and by the level of education. It is conventional wisdom that graduate students need relatively little in-person interaction, whereas younger students (especially K–12) require more.

A practical factor to be considered in requiring on-campus activities is the cost and inconvenience for the student. Keeping in mind that students often enroll in online courses from distant locations (especially in the case of foreign students), any on-campus activity could involve substantial travel time and expense. Furthermore, some students take online courses because on-campus courses are problematic in terms of mobility (for example, individuals with disabilities) or work schedules. So, on-campus activities should be minimized and, ideally, offered as options with alternatives for those who do not wish to attend.

Indeed, there is a growing trend to eliminate all on-campus activities from online programs. In order to do this, the online environment needs to be quite sophisticated, providing all the functions that would normally be conducted on campus—registration, counseling, book ordering, financial aid, and so on. It also needs to address nonacademic functions such as clubs, support groups, and service organizations. Clearly, some functions, such as sports, parties, and eating, have no online counterpart (for better or worse). We will discuss the broader implications of this trend toward totally online programs later in the book.

Almost everything a teacher needs or wants to know about creating Web sites can be found online. The WebTeacher (http://www.webteacher.org) provides an introduction to the Web.

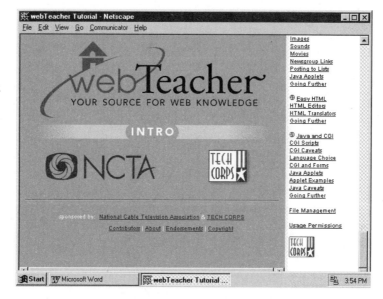

Authoring Courses

At the end of Chapter 3, we briefly discussed authoring tools for creating online courses. The most commonly used authoring tool for most teachers will be a word processing program because the primary course documents (syllabuses, lesson plans, study guides) are text files. Since the current versions of all word processing programs allow documents to be saved in HTML format, creating Web documents does not require any special effort. If these documents involve graphics, photographs, or slide shows, additional software tools will be required, but these are standard application programs that any computer user can be expected to learn. If the institution provides instructional support services, such additional components may be created for the instructor by graphic designers or multimedia specialists.

Courses involving simulations, or using complex interactive sequences for testing or exercises, may require actual programming, using languages such as C, Perl, Visual Basic, or Java. Such programming would be done by a programmer, not the instructor. Similarly, if animations or multimedia sequences are desired, they would be developed by multimedia developers using appropriate software and production hardware. It is possible for instructors to learn how to create these more advanced features, but few would have the inclination or time to do so. One interesting development is the emergence of Java applet collections, which include small instructional programs that can be downloaded and incorporated into Web pages (for example, see the Educational Object Exchange at http://www.eoe.org).

Most of the course delivery environments now in use (for example, WebCt, BlackBoard, LearningSpace, TopClass, FirstClass) provide editing capabilities for the setup of discussion forums, file uploading/downloading areas, student records, class schedules, and grade reporting. This means that the organization and layout of the course interface can be handled by instructors if they desire. However, in most cases, a course administrator will handle these tasks in consultation with the instructor at the beginning of the semester. The course administrator can ensure that the course is set up in accordance with any school or institutional policies and that no critical elements are overlooked.

One Web development and delivery tool that has become very popular is RealMedia from RealNetworks, Inc. (http://www.real.com). RealMedia is a set of Web application programs that allow multimedia segments (audio or video) to be downloaded in small bursts (called streaming media), making it possible to run them even when bandwidth is limited (for example, on dial-up lines using 28.8 modems). One version of the RealMedia tools allows slideshows to be narrated and both slides and audio to be downloaded together. Instructors often use RealMedia presentations to deliver short lectures or tutorials. Business people use RealMedia to deliver briefings and conference presentations as part of virtual meetings.

Probably the biggest problem area in developing online courses is not their initial creation, but subsequent revisions and updating. Even if the content of a course doesn't require much change, many small details, such as dates, references, URLs, and names, will need to be revised. Sometimes is it is difficult to locate the original course files (what machine and hard drive were they done on?) or figure out how they are organized. In many cases, the person revising and teaching the course next is different from the originator. For all these reasons, it is highly desirable to have course files maintained by a single individual (such as the course administrator) on one system using standard formats. In many educational settings, this may seem like an unattainable dream, but it can be accomplished.

For more about the development of Web-based courses, see Duchastel (19996/97), Khan (1997), or McCormack and Jones (1997). Prior to the development of online courses, it is useful to study the design of existing courses (for example, http://www.concord.org/library/review.html, http://snow.utoronto.ca/best/crsreview.html, or http://home.sprynet.com/~gkearsley/allen.htm).

Course Quality

All of the factors we have discussed in this and the preceding chapters are ingredients of good-quality online courses. Here is a brief summary of the ten most critical elements:

1. **Content**   Despite all the glitter and gizmos of technology, the single most important aspect of any online course is the content—whether it is relevant, accurate, up-to-date, and compelling. The information provided must be what students need/want to know, it must be valid and credible, and it must have depth/richness.
2. **Pedagogy**   The nature of the learning strategies and activities employed in the course must be appropriate for the subject matter and the student audience. Regardless of the approach, the learning activities must actively engage the student.
3. **Motivation**   Students must be motivated to learn—a function of interesting content and active participation in the course (engagement). Use of graphics and multimedia helps to make course materials more motivating.
4. **Feedback**   Students need to receive timely feedback on their progress—the more the better. Ideally, students can check their course progress at any time.
5. **Coordination/Organization**   The course materials and activities must be well organized and coordinated. Students should be clear about what they have to do, when, where, and why.
6. **Usability**   All aspects of any online course should be easy to use. This element is simple to state but often difficult to achieve.
7. **Assistance**   Assistance should be available—both online and off-line (phone, in-person)—for problems with content, technology, or logistics.
8. **Assessment**   Grading and evaluation policies/procedures for all course activities and assignments should be explicitly described and adhered to.
9. **Workload**   The number and nature of course assignments should be appropriate for the type and level of course.
10. **Flexibility**   Students have differing interests, backgrounds, and abilities. The course should accommodate these variations by providing choices/options in learning activities and assessment.

Ironically, most of these factors have little to do with computers or networks—they apply just as much to conventional instruction as online courses!

Conclusion

Creating online courses can be very simple or quite complex, depending on the scale of the effort and the authoring tools available. A course developed for individual use in a single school by one teacher will involve a different level of effort than a course to be taken by thousands of people in a large organization. In the latter case certainly, a well-established development methodology should be followed to ensure quality control and minimize costs. In any course design, a balance must be achieved between usability and aesthetics; the ideal course will function well and be attractive.

Because of the range of skills required, online courses are normally developed by small teams that involve instructional designers, multimedia specialists, programmers, and system analysts working together with the instructor or subject-matter expert. Critical course documents to be developed include syllabuses, lesson plans, study guides, and an instructional specification. These principal course documents can be created using a word processing program, which is the primary authoring tool needed for creating online courses. Many other software tools may be needed, but they are likely to be used by members of the development team other than the instructor.

Creating online courses is really no different from developing any other instructional materials—it requires a blend of creativity, ambition, self-discipline, and teamwork to produce a successful product. Indeed, the factors that determine the quality of online courses are the same as with conventional classes.

Judi Harris: Telementoring

Judi Harris is a professor in the College of Education at the University of Texas, Austin. Her focus is on teaching teachers how to use the Internet in the classroom, and she has written a number of guidebooks on this topic published by ITSE and ASCD. She also directs the Electronic Emissary project, an effort to connect students and subject-matter experts via the Internet. She considers this project to be an example of telementoring.

For more about Judi Harris, see http://www.edb.utexas.edu/coe/depts/ci/it/harris.html. The home page for the Electronic Emissary project is http://www.tapr.org/emissary/index.html.

Key Ideas

- Course development can be more effective if it follows a well-defined instructional methodology such as ISD or minimalism.
- Online courses must have good form (aesthetics) and function (usability).
- A team approach is normally needed in the development of online courses.
- Course documents such as syllabuses, lesson plans, and study guides help to organize online courses.
- Integrating online courses with on-campus activities depends on the nature of the learning involved.
- The authoring process for online courses involves a variety of different tools, designed for instructors, programmers, and system administrators.
- Some critical aspects of course quality are content, pedagogy, motivation, feedback, organization, usability, assistance, assessment, workload, and flexibility.

Questions for Further Reflection

1. Can any teacher create a good online course?
2. What do you consider to be the most difficult aspect of creating an online course?
3. What factors affect how long it takes to create an online course?
4. Of the two development methodologies described (ISD and minimalism), which one appeals to you more?
5. Do you believe that most courses can be delivered completely online? What aspects need to be done on-campus?
6. What is the role of an editor in the development of online courses?

8 Organizations and Networking

After completing this chapter, you should understand

- the organizational changes that online education entails in terms of facilities, jobs, policies, procedures, and leadership

- how online education affects the relationships among institutions

In our view, the actual uses and consequences of developing computer systems depend upon the way the world works. Conversely, computerized systems may slowly, but inexorably, change that way—often with unforeseen consequences. A key issue is how to understand the social opportunities and dilemmas of computerization without becoming seduced by the social simplifications of utopian romance or discouraged by anti-utopian nightmares. Both kinds of images are far too simplified. (Dunlop & Kling, 1996, p. 29)

In earlier chapters, we discussed the changes that online education brings for individual students and teachers. However, even greater change is involved for educational institutions and organizations with educational functions (such as training departments). Online education means new roles and re-sponsibilities, new policies and procedures, and may result in new missions and goals. It is no accident that the introduction of technology often occurs simultaneously with institutional restructuring.

In this chapter, we examine some of the organizational ramifications of online education, including changes to physical facilities and staffing, pat-terns of study/work, power relationships, and competition/cooperation among institutions.

Physical Facilities and Support Staff

Let's begin our discussion with one of the more mundane yet fundamental aspects of organizational change brought on by network technology: how it affects physical facilities and infrastructure. In order to participate in online activities, all students and staff need easy access to networked computers. For on-campus access, this normally means computers in offices and labs con-nected to LANs, which in turn have a high-speed connection to the Internet (such as a T1 line). In addition, computers in dormitories, libraries, and classrooms will also need to connect to the LAN (or have their own LANs). Creating this kind of on-campus network means that each machine must have an appropriate LAN interface card, the necessary cable must run through the buildings, and the LAN computers must have software for the LAN and Internet configurations. Printers and various storage devices will need to be connected to different computers in the network. And multimedia adds further considerations (see Szuprowicz, 1995).

To make things more complicated, most students and staff will want to access the institution's system from their homes, using their own computers. This means that the system will need to have dial-up ports that allow users to

In many cases, networking vendors are the best sources of up-to-date technical information, as at the 3Com site (http://www.3com.com/edu).

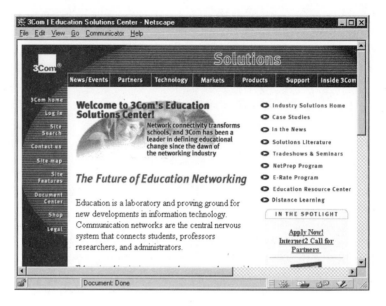

connect via a telephone call, using a variety of different telecommunications programs. As more and more students and staff get involved in online courses, the need to support remote users connecting via telephone dial-up becomes significant and may require hundreds of ports and many phone lines in a large educational institution. Requiring users to have ISP accounts is one way to minimize this problem, because it reduces the need for so many dial-up connections at the institution. When multimedia and desktop video applications are used, providing sufficient bandwidth for remote users is a major problem.

Use of a network tends to raise additional computing issues such as security, virus protection, backups, and file sharing. Although all of these issues pertain to stand-alone computer use, once people are connected to a network, they take on a different context. For example, people rarely worry about someone "breaking in" to their computer when they are stand-alone; however, once connected to a network, they are immediately concerned about "hackers" gaining remote access to their files. Similarly, private access to information on one computer is quite a different matter from public access to information on a server. So, a whole host of issues needs to be addressed once people become network users (see Denning & Denning, 1998; Neumann, 1995).

Installing and supporting all of these network facilities takes considerable staff and money. In the case of small school systems, the lack of both can present major obstacles to networking. The cost of multiple phone lines is a

Some vendors, such as NetSchools (http://www.netschools.net), offer complete educational network solutions, reducing the level of technical expertise required by schools.

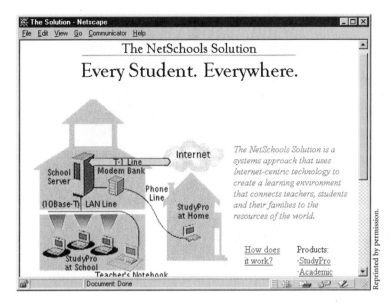

The NetSchools Solution is a systems approach that uses Internet-centric technology to create a learning environment that connects teachers, students and their families to the resources of the world.

How does it work?

Products:
·StudyPro
·Academic

Reprinted by permission.

big problem for some school systems. The U.S. Telecommunications Act of 1996 includes a subsidy program (the "E-rate") that is supposed to reduce the cost of telecommunications services to schools; however, this subsidy has had little practical effect to date (see http://www.slcfund.org). Finding qualified staff is an equally significant concern. School districts may only have one or two network technicians or systems engineers to implement and run their networks. Even in the case of large institutions, such as universities and corporations, having sufficient network staff is frequently a limitation to smooth network operation.

In addition to network technicians, support staff are also needed to help users get connected and troubleshoot problems. Whenever people add new hardware or software to their systems, they are likely to need help reconfiguring it for the network. Novices who are new to computers or network applications will need orientation and training. Basic orientation and training are usually handled through workshops and seminars, but in some cases they require one-on-one attention. Many commercially available self-study courses, some online and some in CD-ROM format, are designed to teach people the basics of operating systems and application programs. Many corporations encourage employees to use such courses to meet their computer literacy needs.

To summarize, providing network capabilities within an organization involves a number of considerations associated with physical facilities and infrastructure, including space for equipment, wiring in buildings, telephone

Finding a good Internet service provider (ISP) is a critical aspect of online education. The List site (http://www.thelist. com) can help with this decision.

connections, support staff, and user training/procedures. An extensive amount of planning, with participation by many parties (users, facilities staff, vendors), will be needed. All of this requires a great deal of administrative time and attention.

Patterns of Study and Work

Online education provides a lot of flexibility in terms of where and when people work, especially if asynchronous interaction is involved. In the case of students, studying and class participation can be done at home in the evenings or on weekends. Similarly, faculty do not need to be on campus to do their teaching—they can do it from home according to their own work schedule. It is also possible for people to study or work while they are traveling, confined to a hospital, or even on vacation—provided they have a computer and access to a phone line.

This flexibility in the location of study or teaching reduces the importance of traditional educational facilities such as classrooms, libraries, offices, and meeting rooms. In theory, a school that used online education extensively would not need the kind of facilities that a traditional institution must have—or related services such as parking, cafeterias, and gymnasiums. So, the fact that students and faculty work off campus at locations of their own choosing means that the educational institution can be operated with fewer physical facilities of its own, reducing overhead costs. At the same time, additional resources must be devoted to computer and network facilities, as discussed in the preceding section.

Because staff and students are on campus less, it becomes more difficult to schedule in-person activities, which reinforces the need for electronic contact. In this way, the move toward online interaction perpetuates more online interaction. The scheduling of on-campus meetings and classes must be formalized, because casual get-togethers (bumping into somebody in a hallway) are less likely to occur. Paradoxically, people can have a higher level of contact once they move to online interaction (email, conferencing), even though they have less in-person interaction. Because it is relatively easy to include additional people in an email message or conference connection, the chances are higher that more group communication will take place online than in traditional settings.

One weak area for online interaction, however, is supervision and management. Most individuals who have supervisory or management responsibilities over others (deans, department heads, principals, thesis advisers) are not comfortable conducting such activities entirely in electronic form. Although it is very easy to track the work of someone via online means (for example, log-on records, file or screen sharing), it is usually considered difficult to solve disputes or conflicts this way. Most people prefer to handle these aspects of supervision and management through in-person meetings. It is also difficult to get an overall picture of a person's progress or state of being solely from online interaction. Consequently, most supervisors and managers like to have periodic in-person meetings with their staff, even though most of the actual work can be done online.

The fact that students and staff do not have to be on campus all the time changes patterns of transportation, shopping, and community services. Less commuting from home to school is needed, and shopping is more likely to be done close to home rather than near school. Alternatively, individuals may take advantage of online services for buying books, supplies, or software, reducing their need for local shopping. The need for day-care services may also be reduced if staff and students are able to work from home. Although electronic education is thus likely to have a significant impact on patterns of urban behavior, each local setting will have its own trade-offs, and it is very difficult to predict overall effects.

Many traditional elements of education will undoubtedly be affected. For example, school buses are a fixture of K–12 schooling. However, if a substantial portion of students in a school district take their classes online, the need for busing will be significantly diminished. To the extent that some

Creating an online campus involves defining how students, faculty, and administrative staff will interact. Embanet (http://www.embanet.com) is an example of a commercial service that provides online learning environments.

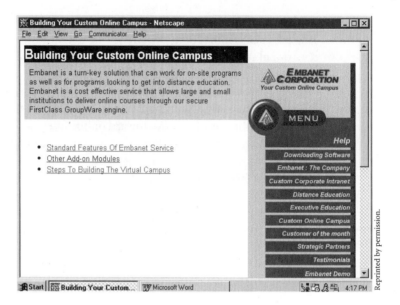

on-campus classes and activities still exist, buses will still be needed, but perhaps to move only small numbers of students, less often, with a more variable time schedule. Similarly affected will be food services, sports and extracurricular activities, and libraries. Making the transition from a full-time, on-campus institution to a part-time, predominantly off-campus one will be difficult for most schools.

Power Relationships

One aspect of organizations that online interaction changes considerably is the relationships of authority and power (see Davenport, 1997; Dunlop & Kling, 1996; Sproull & Kiesler, 1991). When information is communicated through a physical means (including telephone and fax), lines of authority can be maintained through gatekeepers (secretaries and assistants). However, online interaction via email and conferencing tends to override these channels, allowing anyone to contact anyone else. Indeed, in most systems, there is no reason why a student can't send a message directly to a principal or provost (if they can discover their email identity). Likewise, a staff member in one department can contact staff in another department (or perhaps all staff in the organization) without going through supervisors or administrators. Furthermore, online messages all look the same, with no indicators of position or prestige. Within an online class, each student has the same voice as the instructor; there is no dominant position at the front of the classroom. Online interaction is a true equalizer with respect to power and usurps the traditional authority role of the teacher or manager.

As a consequence of this phenomenon, individuals within organizations tend to be recognized for their competence (as displayed by their online activities) rather than according to traditional measures of seniority or position. Staff who are very knowledgeable or especially helpful to others online are heavily consulted and gain good reputations within the organization. (This also happens in courses among students.) Conversely, those who have no online presence lose authority within the organization, even if they have it on paper. The chain of command tends to follow the communication patterns of an organization, which take on new pathways with electronic interaction.

As more functions go online, people with good network skills and knowledge become more valuable to the organization. For example, most large organizations now have a CIO (chief information officer) position with responsibilities and authority at least as important to the well-being of the organization as those of the traditional CEO (chief executive officer) and CFO (chief financial officer) roles. Similarly, in a university or school system, the director of computer or information services is usually very influential. Almost every activity of a modern organization or institution is affected by its computer systems and networks; whoever oversees this function makes decisions that impact everyone.

Thus, individuals with online expertise and capability (whether staff or students) wield considerable power in contemporary organizations. But computer system virtuosity alone does not make a good leader. Leaders must be able to motivate people, articulate visions and goals, create coalitions, develop strategies, problem-solve, and above all, communicate well. As it turns out, online activities can facilitate many of these leadership functions, particularly those having to do with planning, discussion, and communication. For individuals who have leadership capability, online environments offer the chance to be even more effective, if they master networking. It should come as no surprise that most leaders today seek out assistants or technical staff who have networking expertise.

Centralization/Decentralization

One of the enduring issues in large organizations is the centralization/decentralization of functions. This issue is just as applicable to school and college systems as it is to companies and government agencies. Once again, networks are a key element, because they can be used to facilitate centralization or decentralization, usually through database access—that is, who creates and controls financial information or student records—but also through sharing of curriculum or computing resources.

Historically, networks have been used to centralize functions and achieve economies of scale. For example, most educational institutions use computer-based systems for key administrative functions such as student registration, course listings, classroom scheduling, budgets, and payroll. The software runs on a central host, and all departments are expected to enter their data remotely. Because of the cost of the software, as well as the training required to use it, this model made sense. However, this model means that all decisions are made centrally, with little access to the data by the contributing departments.

In the past decade, organizational/institutional restructuring efforts have placed much more emphasis on site-based management and departmental autonomy. As administrative software became less expensive and easier to use, it became reasonable for individual schools or departments to have their own copies of registration, scheduling, student management, or financial processing programs. Data could be processed and analyzed locally, then passed on to a centralized entity (the school district, the dean's office, corporate headquarters) for aggregation. In some cases, the software still resides on a central host, but it processes data stored locally.

The issues underlying the centralization/decentralization question are flexibility and control. If individual sites have the ability to process their own data, they can design the data collection or analysis to meet their needs. For example, a school may want to ask some additional questions in its student registration system that would not routinely be included in a general system. Alternatively, a school may want to perform some data analyses that would not normally be done. However, in allowing sites this measure of flexibility, the central administration gives up some degree of control over the way the system is used. And since control is a manifestation of power and authority, giving up control will likely alter the power relationships in an organization. To relate this point back to the topic of networks, the way networks are designed, in terms of centralized or decentralized functions, affects the structure of power in the organization.

Cooperation and Competition

One of the most intriguing aspects of online education is how it affects the relationships among institutions, in terms of cooperation and competition. Just as networking can facilitate collaboration among students or faculty, it can also do so at the institutional level. The most obvious form of collabora-

Many institutions are joining consortiums to offer online courses—for example, the California Virtual University (http://www.california.edu).

tion is course sharing, in which a group of institutions agree to jointly offer online courses to their respective student populations. In the usual case, each institution will offer existing courses that collectively make up a degree, certificate, or extension program. Students pay tuition to the institution that they take the course from, so there is revenue sharing across the participants. Since online courses have no geographical boundaries, any group of institutions can collaborate. Many groups of institutions have formed consortiums to serve as the administrative framework for these offerings. Examples include the Western Governors University (http://www.wgu.edu), the California Virtual University (http://www.california.edu), and the Southern Regional Electronic Campus (http://www.srec.sreb.org).

Clearly this idea has many advantages. Each school can leverage its particular expertise and course offerings to a larger potential pool of students. Equally important, schools don't have to try to develop and offer every course needed by their students. This advantage is particularly significant in subject areas where faculty are scarce. Intellectually, students and staff benefit from exposure to a wider range of ideas and perspectives, especially when schools from different nations are involved. Finally, administrative and network resources may be shared, producing better capabilities than any single institution could provide.

Alas, this collaborative model often runs counter to some basic human characteristics: greed and pride. Some institutions (particularly the larger,

Many publishing and media organizations are using online learning to extend their markets. The PBS TeacherSource site (http://www.pbs.org) links public television with the classroom.

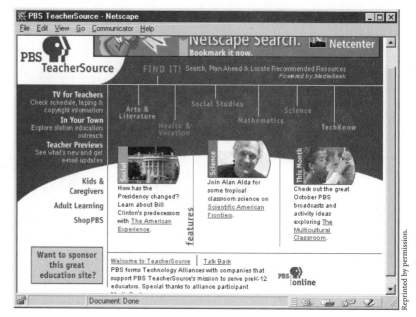

more established ones) are not satisfied with sharing a student population with other schools. They want all of the students and their tuition revenue, and they see no need to share courses if the institution can do it all. Some schools also believe that they can do it better than any others—that they can develop and offer superior courses on their own. They may feel that other schools offer "second-rate" teaching that will diminish the value of their students' learning experience. Since there are no objective measures of academic standards in higher education, it is hard to address this issue.

Al Rogers: Linking Kids Around the World

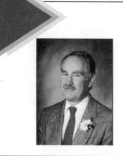

Al Rogers is a former classroom teacher who has played a prominent role in getting students online around the world. Along with his partner, Yvonne Marie Andres, he developed FrEdMail (and the FrEdWriter program), which provided a low-cost email system for schools. Currently he is the executive director of the Global SchoolNet Foundation (http://www.gsn.org), which supports a number of projects for online interaction among schools and students in many different nations.

The corporate world is not inclined toward cooperative training programs because much training is proprietary in nature and sharing across companies is undesirable. However, trade associations, which represent the interests of all organizations in a given industry sector, are good candidates to develop online courses with contributions and participation from member companies. Although companies many not be eager to partner directly with each other, they are usually enthusiastic about partnerships with schools, thus providing an excellent domain for online courses. Because online courses do not require travel and study can be done at work or home, they fit employee needs very well. Many universities and colleges have developed online programs in management and technical skill areas that specifically meet the needs of certain corporations or industries.

Finally, we should mention the many private initiatives that are taking place in the online education world. Companies are creating "virtual schools" that offer degree or certificate programs. Some of these companies are subsidiaries of publishing or media organizations that see online education as an extension of their existing businesses. Others come from the education groups of major corporations that see online courses as a way to leverage their training efforts. Some are spin-offs from existing educational institutions, intended to be profit-making. All of these enterprises provide competition to traditional institutions, which can choose to ignore them, form some kind of partnership, or compete directly in the online education business.

Conclusion

In this chapter, we have discussed some of the organizational implications of networks, including physical facilities and support staff, changes in work/study patterns, effects on power relationships, and cooperation/competition among institutions. This discussion only scratches the surface of the many changes that networking can bring to an organization. By changing the way people interact, networking affects every aspect of how an organization functions. More than just another communication function added to those that already exist (such as telephone and fax), networking entails a structural change in the way an organization works. Online education doesn't merely add new capabilities to schools; it transforms them into new institutions.

In the next chapter, we will look at the effects of networks on educational policy: the interface between schools and other elements of the society in which they function.

For more discussion about networks and their future impact on organizations, see Dizard (1997), Doheny-Farina (1996), or Miller (1996).

Key Ideas

- Online education involves many changes and additions to physical facilities and support staff.
- Online education is likely to change the patterns of study and work.
- Online education will affect the power relationships in an institution.
- Online education create new opportunities for collaboration as well as competition among institutions.

Questions for Further Reflection

1. Why is it easier to equip a new school for networking than to add networking to an existing school?
2. What is the likely impact on the power structure of a school when networking is implemented?
3. How do personal relationships in a class change as a result of online interaction?
4. What factors determine how much on-campus time is needed for a given course or program of study?
5. Which institutions have more to gain or lose from collaborative arrangements for online teaching?
6. What are the pros and cons for an institution considering whether to provide online courses and programs?

9

Policy

After completing this chapter, you should understand

- issues associated with ownership, quality control, and access of online course materials

- implications of online courses for institutional policies

Ease of use seems to be the subtext in a number of discussions about trouble-some materials on the Internet. Parents will claim that pornographic materials, bomb recipes, and so on, are, in a sense, being broadcast directly into their homes. It is not like the old days when Junior had to cross the tracks and go to the other side of town to find such materials. (Ludlow, 1996, p. 254)

Picture this scenario. It's 8 P.M. on a weekday night and your 12-year-old child suddenly remembers he has a major school report on the Spanish-American War due tomorrow. He needs to do some research, but the library is closed. No problem! Your cyber-savvy youngster simply turns on your computer, activates your modem, logs on to the Internet—the revolutionary "Information Super-highway"—and, in a matter of minutes, is exchanging pictures of naked women with other youngsters all over North America. (Barry, 1996, p. 13)

In the previous chapter, we discussed the organizational impact of online education. Many of the issues raised in that context, as well as earlier in the book, involve broader policy concerns. Among these broader concerns are ownership of electronic materials, quality control of online courses, student/faculty workloads, certification and accreditation, and acceptable use. This last issue encompasses fundamental questions about freedom of speech, privacy, and censorship.

Ownership

In theory, questions of ownership (which include copyright, royalties, and licensing) are no different for online materials than any other media. Educational institutions often specify in their employment contracts that all instructional materials developed by faculty or staff are the exclusive property of the institution. Copyright law clearly spells out the rules of ownership for works in electronic form (for example, Cavazos & Morin, 1994). And today's publishing contracts normally outline in extraordinary detail the terms for royalties and licensing of all materials, including electronic versions.

But online courses raise questions of ownership that are difficult to answer. For example, if a document consists primarily of links to other Web sites, who is the owner of the material used when the document is read and the links activated? At present, placing a link to another site does not require permission or royalty payments for access. Yet the linked document itself represents a unique work that can be copyrighted. Of course, if material from another site is actually copied and reproduced, that does require permission

The Copyright Website (http:// www.benedict. com).

and/or royalties, as with any medium. An additional complication is that online works are increasingly the product of international collaborations, but copyright laws (and the degree of their enforcement) vary across nations.

Even though contracts may specify that all materials developed by faculty or staff belong to the institution, most teachers believe that they have personal ownership, as in the case of a book or paper they have written. Teachers are less likely to take this view when course materials are developed by a team and no single individual can claim sole authorship. Historically, it has been difficult for institutions to exert their ownership rights over course materials because they are so difficult to keep track of. However, with online materials stored on a school server, it is easier to maintain ownership by controlling access to the server and the files it contains. When people leave an organization, they may lose access to the system and materials. Faculty need to be careful about what documents they store on which systems. Personal documents should be kept on a personal account, not an institutional one. Doing so also finesses questions of institutional censorship, to be discussed later in the chapter. Of course, keeping materials on separate systems does not alleviate fraud or theft on the part of individuals with respect to institutional ownership.

In previous chapters, we have discussed collaboration among faculty at different institutions in developing and delivering online courses. Collaboration of this sort is problematic as far as ownership is concerned. An easy way out is for one of the institutions to have ownership, if the other schools involved are willing to accept this arrangement (not likely). An alternative solution is to have a third party, such as a publishing company or a consortium, have ownership. The situation is even more complicated when state-funded schools are involved, because it can be argued that the materials are public domain (or at least owned by the state).

An additional wrinkle in the ownership of online course materials is student contributions. Assuming that an engagement model of learning is practiced, with much of the course material coming from student assignments, what ownership rights should students have? In the past, student-generated materials did not constitute a significant component of course materials, but this is likely to change with online courses. Should students be viewed as contributors and given suitable credit and compensation?

Quality Control

One of the concerns that is shared by most faculty and administrators (as well as the public) about online courses is whether the quality of education is on a par with that of traditional on-campus classes. Research on the effectiveness of online courses, reviewed in Chapter 4, suggests that they can be just as effective, or more so, in terms of learning outcomes. But that research doesn't address the question of whether a particular course is good. Educational institutions need to develop quality control procedures that ensure the effectiveness of all online courses they offer.

Quality control of courses is not something that most schools do well. Ensuring the effectiveness of courses is something normally left to faculty and addressed by end-of-course student evaluation questionnaires. Such questionnaires are not usually very illuminating, and the data they do provide are often not taken into account in revising courses. Furthermore, these data come at the end of the course, when it is too late to make any changes for the current students. Corporations and government agencies tend to do a better job of quality control, because the outcome of training (satisfactory job performance) is important to organizational effectiveness (see Baker & O'Neil, 1994).

Some institutions have evaluation groups (typically part of their instructional support services) that seek to conduct more rigorous and meaningful quality control efforts. These efforts include carrying out pilot and field tests of newly developed courses, asking students to identify problems and weak elements. One of the most important aspects of such initial testing is to determine if the content and activities correspond to the instructional objectives or goals of the course. More often than not, there will be missing or irrelevant

The Electronic Frontier Foundation (EFF) is an organization dedicated to the examination of network policy issues (http://www.eff.org).

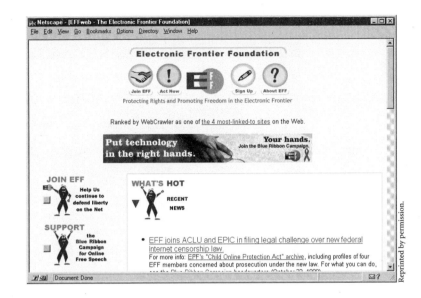

content and learning activities that do not help to achieve the desired outcomes of the course. For this kind of evaluation to be done properly, it must be performed by an objective party—not the instructor, subject-matter expert, or course author, who have too much self-involvement to make a neutral assessment.

Follow-up of learning achievement after course completion is critical to quality control. In many cases, it is difficult to determine if a course was effective until students are trying to apply the skills or knowledge in jobs or subsequent courses. The engagement model outlined in Chapter 5 makes course assessment easier because students are asked to apply what they are learning in real-world contexts during the course. Follow-up studies involve asking students, as well as their supervisors and coworkers, if the skills and knowledge acquired in their courses have enabled them to do their job proficiently (and if not, what the deficiencies are).

Nothing that has been said up to this point about quality control has anything specifically to do with online courses. However, the online environment does make it easier to interact with students and collect data. Questionnaires can be administered online and the results collected and tabulated automatically. As students are going through the material, they can make comments in the form of online notes that are immediately available to evaluators. Ideally, students will be interviewed while they are studying, because this is when their observations are most accurate. With online learning, it may be possible to observe directly what students are doing via screen

The Western Interstate Commission for Higher Education (WICHE) is a regional organization that focuses on policy issues for higher education (http://www.wiche.edu).

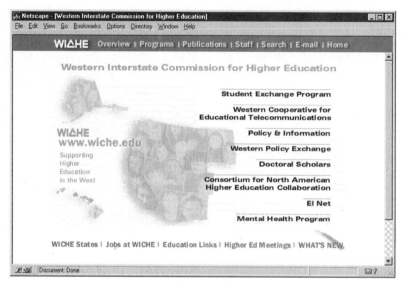

monitoring (with permission of the students involved). Follow-up studies can be done via email, discussion forums, or conferencing. So, online evaluation makes data collection easier and faster, but it does not radically change the nature of the quality control process.

Student/Faculty Workloads

Among the data items that can be collected as part of the quality control process are how much time students spend studying and how much time faculty spend teaching. These data are especially important with online courses for a number of reasons. For one thing, schools (and accrediting bodies) have certain expectations about how many hours of study are required to complete a course for a certain number of credits. In traditional on-campus instruction, it is easy to determine the number of hours that students spend in class (assuming they attend). But how are attendance and number of hours of study to be determined in an online class?

Actually, it turns out to be easy to measure the amount of online time because this is automatically recorded by the system. Almost any online system can produce records of student sign-on time as well as what they did while they were signed on (such as number and type of responses). To the extent that students send email, participate in conferences, and post messages in discussion forums, all of these activities can be tabulated or kept as records

The Consortium for Policy Research in Education (http://www.upenn.edu/gse/cpre/).

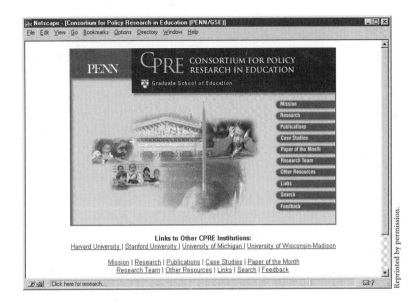

of student performance. Of course, these records don't indicate that learning is taking place any more than when a student is occupying a seat in a classroom. But they do indicate that students are actively participating in the course.

Although it possible that the student workload in an online course is too light for the designated credit hours, in most cases it is too heavy. Teachers are inclined to give assignments involving online collaboration, research, or writing that are very time-consuming, without realizing how long it takes to complete these assignments. For those following the engagement model, projects may require an enormous amount of background work that is difficult to gauge from the finished product (unless it is documented). When students are asked to track and report the amount of time they spend studying and completing assignments for online courses, the numbers are often many times more than for on-campus classes. However, these numbers normally include time spent learning and using the online system, which can be appreciable for novices and newcomers.

The way faculty usually discover that the student workload is too high (apart from student complaints) is when they review assignments and realize how much time students are spending on their coursework. Furthermore, there is a relationship between student and faculty workload: a high student workload (many assignments) will normally translate into a high teacher workload (many assignments to be graded). This is not simply a matter of numbers, but also the complexity of the responses and hence the time needed to grade them. So, just as online courses typically have higher student workloads than on-campus courses, they also have higher faculty workloads. In Chapter 6, we discussed strategies for coping with the higher workloads of online courses.

Assuming that student and faculty workloads are higher for online courses (and are not adjusted), this raises questions about increasing the value of these courses in terms of credits and load factors. Should two online courses be equivalent to three on-campus courses? Should the duration of online courses be lengthened to stretch out the workload over a longer time period? Team efforts in taking or teaching these courses could also spread out the workload, although this is not normally taken into account in determining student credits or teaching loads.

The workload issue is just as relevant to workplace training and home learning as it is to the school environment. Online training that requires too much time will simply not get done, no matter how relevant or important it is to the employee. It is especially important when developing and delivering online training to break all learning activities and materials into small chunks so they can fit into busy work or personal schedules. Similarly, online learning materials designed for the home environment should not require extensive involvement or supervision by parents, who typically have limited time/patience for teaching. If the learning activities engage the students properly, they should not need a lot of attention from parents; instead, they should be interacting with other students and online resources.

The Education Commission of the States (ECS) coordinates educational policy nationally (http://www.ecs.org).

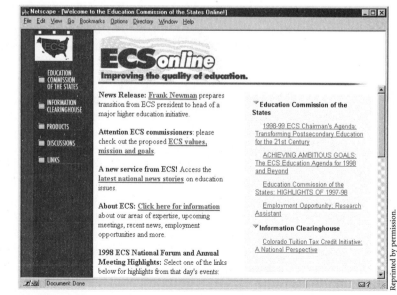

The American Council for Education (http://www.acenet.edu) provides accreditation guidelines for post-secondary learning.

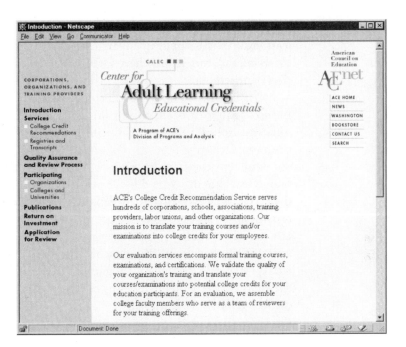

Accreditation and Certification

Some of the issues we have been discussing in preceding sections provide the background to questions about the accreditation of online programs and the certification of those who teach online. Given the common concern with the quality of online courses, it is no surprise that the credentials of those who teach and the institutions that offer such courses are subjected to additional scrutiny. Likewise, to the extent that course workloads are related to credits and learning outcomes, there is a connection between accreditation and the nature of online courses.

In the United States, certification of K–12 teachers is a state-level function. To teach in a given state requires certification for that state. In theory, if an online course involved students from different states, the teacher would need to be certified in every state. Indeed, some teachers have actually done this for classes delivered by interactive video. But clearly such multiple credentials are not feasible on a large scale. Online teaching will require changes in certification regulations that allow credentials to be recognized across state lines.

Note that certification is only required at the K–12 level; college faculty do not need any kind of credentials (other than graduate degrees). However, institutions of higher education are accredited by regional accreditation bodies. Accreditation bodies want evidence that courses involve adequate learning activities. Online courses tend to be difficult for most examiners to assess because they usually have little personal experience with online education. Consequently, extra effort is often needed to describe the learning activities in online courses and document the outcomes, making the accreditation process more complex for institutions that offer such courses. This situation should change over time as online education becomes more commonplace.

Another side of this issue is how to determine if teachers are qualified for online teaching. It's very difficult to predict if instructors will do well with online teaching even though they may have an excellent record in traditional classroom settings. No teacher credentials include online teaching competencies. Indeed, very few teacher preparation programs at present include any substantial exposure to online teaching. The best-qualified teachers are those who have completed training programs that involve online courses. Although they may not have online teaching experience, at least they are familiar with the nature of online learning.

Acceptable Use

One of the most complex policy issues associated with the Internet and computer networks is acceptable use—regulating what is acceptable online behavior. Acceptable use covers what kinds of information can be accessed and stored online, and by whom. It also covers how online facilities are used. Almost every educational institution has its own acceptable use policy that all students are expected to abide by, with penalties for violations. However, the dilemma with defining acceptable use is that the various groups concerned (students, faculty, administrators, parents) are likely to have differing opinions about what online activities/information should be permitted and prohibited, and these opinions will vary considerably across individuals.

The most contentious of all acceptable use issues is censorship—limitations on access to certain sites, normally those containing sexually explicit material. Schools and parents do not want children to be able to access pornographic materials or participate in sexually oriented online discussions. Indeed, this concern is so widespread in the United States that the U.S. Congress has passed laws, including the 1998 Child Online Decency Act, that attempt to regulate commercial providers. However, civil libertarians decry any efforts to limit access to online sites, regardless of their content. Most schools (and parents) try to deal with this potential problem by close monitoring of what students do in computer labs or by installing "filter" programs that block access to "banned" sites. Another potential strategy is to provide

The Virginia Department of Education has created an AUP Handbook (http://www.pen.k12.va.us/go/VDOE/Technology/AUP/home.shtml) that is a useful resource for creating an AUP.

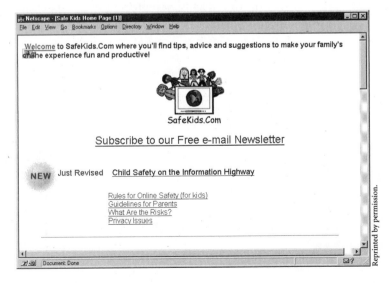

different levels of access for different students, depending upon age and parental wishes.

A second aspect of appropriate use is adhering to software licensing and copyright laws. A classic problem in educational settings is student piracy of software programs. This problem has been addressed by school licensing arrangements that allow all students at an institution to use specified programs. In addition, the software provided in most school computers labs is

The SafeKids Web site (http://www.safekids.com) provides guidance on how to ensure a wholesome online experience for children.

The EdWeb site created by Andy Carvin (http://edweb.gsn.org) discusses the policy implications of online education.

```
Netscape - [EdWeb Home Page]                                    _ □ ×
File  Edit  View  Go  Bookmarks  Options  Directory  Window  Help
```

EdWeb
Exploring Technology and School Reform
by Andy Carvin

© Graphics Only: Copyright 1998 Corporation for Public Broadcasting. All rights reserved.

Latest Revision: October 16, 1998

Named by NetGuide Magazine as One of the 50 Best Places to Go Online!

WELCOME TO EDWEB, written and produced by Andy Carvin. The purpose of this hyperbook is to explore the worlds of educational reform and information technology. With EdWeb, you can hunt down on-line educational resources around the world, learn about trends in education policy and information infrastructure development, examine success stories of computers in the classroom, and much, much more. EdWeb is a dynamic work-in-progress, and numerous changes and additions occur on a regular basis.

To begin, please enter the EdWeb Home Room. To speed up your access, please select the Home Room nearest you:

```
    64% of 7K
```

locked and cannot be copied. However, many students are still inclined to copy programs from one another instead of purchasing them, and piracy remains a problem. Similarly, students may use material they find online (text passages, graphics, music) in their own work without obtaining proper permission to do so. Given the wealth of material available on the Web and how easy it is to download or copy, it is not too surprising that this is a common problem. Students need to be constantly reminded about plagiarism and the meaning of copyright—a task that all instructors need to perform.

A third aspect of acceptable use is respecting the rights and privacy of others. This dimension of acceptable use includes not harassing other students online in any form and not tampering with the account or files of an-

Jason Ohler: Exploring the Electronic Frontier

Jason Ohler is Director of Educational Technology for the University of Alaska and a longtime advocate of online education. His efforts focus on the creative, effective, and responsible use of technology in education. He is the founder of one of the first online journals about distance education (The Online Chronicle of Distance Education and Communication) and the author of Thinking about Technology (http://ivaldi.jun.alaska.edu/edtech/tat/cover/covfram.html). He is also a musician and composer with interests in computer-based music.

See his home page at http://www2.jun.alaska.edu/edtech/jason_ohler.html.

other student or staff member. Forms of harassment include sending online "hate" mail and online stalking (both of which are illegal acts in the United States and elsewhere), as well as "spamming"—sending unsolicited email messages to large numbers of users. Account tampering includes misrepresenting others in email messages or conference postings—something that is often looked upon as a harmless prank by students. It also includes very serious offenses, such as attempting to access computer systems illegally ("hacking") or creating viruses that disable systems or destroy files, that are likely to lead to criminal prosecution.

Clearly, acceptable use considerations cover a broad range of unacceptable behaviors, some of which have very serious consequences. Underlying all of these considerations are questions of morality and ethics. Such questions are no easier to address in online education than in traditional classrooms. It may be a little easier to monitor and identify unacceptable behavior in online environments because all user actions can be stored and traced. However, such monitoring presents yet another ethical dilemma: respecting the privacy of users in their online activities. This topic will be discussed further in the next chapter.

Conclusion

Online education raises a number of policy issues that have to be addressed by school administrators and the managers of educational organizations, resulting in regulations, guidelines, or procedures for students and staff. In many cases, the issues are so broad in scope (for example, copyright, certification, censorship) that they require the attention of larger bodies, such as government agencies, professional associations, courts, and legislatures. Making online education work depends on solving problems at these levels just as much as on what is taught and how.

Key Ideas

- Ownership policies for online materials must preserve individual and institutional rights without limiting legitimate access.
- Quality control procedures are needed to ensure the effectiveness of online courses.
- Student and faculty workloads for online courses must be monitored, and adjusted if they become too heavy.
- Accreditation and certification issues arise from the uncertainty associated with online courses and teaching.
- Acceptable use policies are a way for institutions to shape online behavior, in terms of content and the nature of interaction.

Questions for Further Reflection

1. Do you think that copyright laws still make sense in the information age?
2. What do you think is the best way to ensure the quality of online courses?
3. What are the consequences of too heavy a workload for students and faculty?
4. Do teacher certification and institutional accreditation really matter for online courses?
5. What do you think are the best ways to ensure acceptable use of computers in education?

10

Education in the Information Age

After completing this chapter, you should understand

- the social, political, and financial issues associated with online education

- the potential impact of virtual schools

*Across the world there is a passionate love affair between children and comput-
ers. I have worked with children and computers in Africa and Asia and
America, in cities, in suburbs, on farms, and in jungles. I have worked with
poor children and rich children; with children of bookish parents and with
children from illiterate families. But these differences don't seem to matter.
Everywhere, with very few exceptions, I see the same gleam in their eyes, the
same desire to appropriate this thing. And more than wanting it, they seem to
know in a deep way it already belongs to them. They know they can master it
more easily and naturally than their parents. They know they are the computer
generation.* (Papert, 1996, p. 1)

Online education has the potential to change fundamentally the way learning, teaching, and schooling take place. But this change has many social, political, and financial implications. Furthermore, a number of questions need
to be raised about technology and its impact on society. This chapter discusses some of these implications and questions.

Access: The Haves and Have-nots

Throughout this book, we have stressed the fact that online education only
works if students and teachers have easy and regular access to computers with
network connections. As a general rule, this is not a problem in the relatively
affluent suburban areas of developed countries. However, the situation is
quite different in the poor urban and rural areas of the world (including the
United States). In these settings, there may be few computers and very limited or no network connections. For such students and teachers, online education is not a possibility at the current time.

There is considerable debate about whether this situation will change
quickly or not. It is not simply a matter of providing suitable computer
equipment (a common initiative of government agencies and technology
companies) because a complex infrastructure consisting of telecommunications links, technical personnel, trained teachers, and a supportive populace
is needed to make online education successful. Parents, teachers, school administrators, and politicians must really want computer-based education in
order for it to happen. Time and time again, computer equipment has been
donated to schools only to be put in storerooms for lack of capability to use
it. Development of the necessary infrastructure usually takes many years,
even in developed nations.

The Rural Education Activities Programme (REAP) in New Zealand is an effort to ensure that individuals in rural areas have online access (http://reap.org.nz).

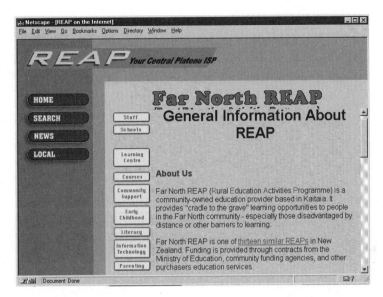

But the issue is even more problematic because poor areas tend to remain poor. Even when the infrastructure is developed and schools in poor areas do manage to get online, they typically have less capable equipment, teachers with limited training, inadequate technical support, and conflicting political/family pressures. So, even when some success is achieved, the gap between the technological haves and have-nots remains wide. Whether this will always remain true, or whether some kind of equalization will eventually be reached, is difficult to predict. For further discussion of these issues, see Bowers (1988), Cummins and Sayers (1995), or Fisher, Dwyer, and Yokam (1996).

Technology: Good or Evil?

A general debate rages over the immediate and long-term desirability of technology: the technophiles versus the technophobes (for example, Dreyfus, 1992; Landauer, 1995; Norman, 1993; Postman, 1992). Many have argued that our increasing reliance on technology is a fatal flaw that will ultimately lead to the demise of society; others see it as the road to utopia. Most people accept it at face value and see neither Armageddon nor utopian implications. The critical question is whether technology is inherently good or evil—or whether it simply reflects the characteristics of the individuals or groups that use it.

In the context of online education, the debate is a little more focused. The primary issue is whether extensive time spent at a computer deprives

The U.S. government has a number of offices that consider the implications of technology—for example, the White House Office of Science and Technology Policy (http://www.whitehouse. gov). For 23 years, the Office of Technology Assessment provided such policy guidance to the U.S. Congress, but this function was disbanded in 1995 (see http://www.wws. princeton.edu/~ota/).

students of worldly contact. Does online learning mean that students lack proper social interaction or actual experience with the flora and fauna of life? Even if they have considerable interaction with others online and much exposure to information, does this provide good socialization and a genuine understanding of the world? At the present time, very few students spend enough time online for these to be serious questions. But in the future, they could be legitimate concerns.

This issue also relates to individual preferences and freedom. Online learning or teaching may not be desirable for all individuals. Some people may never be able to learn or teach via computer. What options will such individuals have if online education becomes the primary choice? Presumably, there will always be schools that offer traditional classes (although class selection may be very limited), and in-person tutoring will certainly be available (though perhaps only privately). So, alternatives will likely exist for those who want to opt out of online education, but they may be quite limited.

Privacy

A more serious issue of individual freedom is privacy in online environments. We have mentioned in earlier chapters that is easy to capture the full details of what a student does while signed on, usually for the legitimate purpose of tracking student performance or providing assistance during learning activities. However, users may not be informed or aware of this automatic

The Electronic Privacy
Information Center
(EPIC) is a good
resource for information
about online privacy
issues (http://epic.org).

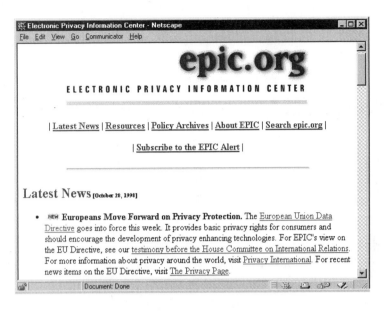

data recording—or be able to do anything about it. For example, it is common for school systems to monitor all online transactions in computer labs, watching for violations of acceptable use policies (such as accessing pornography, spamming, or hacking attempts). Such monitoring may include reading private email messages.

Although almost all institutions and organizations state in their acceptable use policies or employee contracts that they have the right to monitor computer transactions, people are rarely aware that it is done and that they really have no online privacy when using computers on the premises of the institution/organization, or even when using the institution's system from home. The use of a commercial ISP does not ensure privacy either, because they also monitor customer transactions.

In general, the kinds of transactions that occur in the context of an online course are relatively benign and not something that most people would be too concerned about as far as privacy is concerned. But people do sometimes have highly personal discussions via email that would be very embarrassing if made public. And as commercial entities become increasingly involved in online education, the concern becomes greater, because information may be collected for marketing purposes. All individuals are entitled to certain privacy safeguards during online activities, but at present such safeguards do not exist in most educational settings.

One interesting attempt to address these issues is the TRUSTe privacy system (see http://www.truste.org). TRUSTe is a nonprofit consortium that has established some basic privacy rules for Web sites that all members agree to comply with. The consortium reviews member sites for compliance and handles any user complaints. Member sites in good standing display the TRUSTe logo on their Web pages.

Quality of Online Information

An issue that worries many faculty and librarians is the quality of information available on the Web. Because anyone can put up Web documents, there is no peer evaluation process similar to that which forms the foundation for the publication of most scholarly and technical information. Few online journals currently involve a reviewing process, which is usual for printed journals (although this is changing gradually). So the majority of the information found on the Web is raw and unfiltered. Students who use the Web to collect information for projects, papers, or theses may uncritically accept what they find. Given that the Web becomes the primary source of information in online education, this is a significant issue.

To address this concern, some educators are providing their students with lessons and sessions on evaluating the quality of online information, often in conjunction with introductions to the use of search engines. An interesting example of such a program is the Internet Detective, developed at the University of Bristol in the United Kingdom (http://sosig.ac.uk/desire/internet-detective.htm).

Costs and Benefits

Although the benefits of online education have been alluded to from time to time in this book, there has been no direct discussion of costs and benefits. The primary benefit of online courses is that the effort to develop and deliver them can be distributed over a large student audience, resulting in economies of scale for educational institutions. In the case of higher education and private companies, larger student enrollment means more tuition revenue. For public schools and training organizations, larger enrollment lowers the cost per student and hence operating expenses. From the student's perspective, the availability of many online courses from different institutions means a variety of choices in terms of subject matter, instructors, media alternatives, and pricing.

However, there are incremental costs associated with the number of students taking a course. In order to ensure a good level of instructor–student interaction, as well as keep the workload manageable, one teacher can only handle about twenty to thirty students (perhaps less with certain kinds of students or subjects). So, every group of twenty to thirty students in a course requires another instructor or teaching assistant. Certain costs of administering courses and providing technical support also increase proportionately with the number of students. Finally, if the institution is providing the computer equipment used by students, the number of students will directly affect these costs as well (although students will likely share computer resources).

For all these reasons, it is not possible to simply increase the enrollment in an online course without also increasing the budget—although this is not apparent to many administrators. Because no additional classroom or physical facilities are needed, it appears that online classes have infinite expandability. However, the consequences of overloading an online course are that the quality of the learning experience (as indicated by the level of interactivity) quickly deteriorates to the point where students (and faculty) are very dissatisfied, with consequent high attrition, complaints, and poor learning outcomes.

The other major benefit of online courses is that they can lead to more effective learning and teaching. In earlier chapters, we have discussed the potential of the engagement model, as well as the possibilities for global interaction and use of the vast resources the Internet provides. Simulations offer tremendous opportunity for experiential and hands-on learning. Online learning may get students excited about learning who otherwise would drop out of school from boredom. Online courses can make it possible for some individuals to complete degree programs who would not be able to do so with traditional classes. These kinds of benefits are difficult to quantify, except to the extent that they result in more students taking courses and hence higher enrollments. Improved learning/teaching will ultimately mean a better-educated workforce and population, leading to greater productivity and economic prosperity for the nation as a whole.

The costs of the equipment and network connections for online education can be appreciable. Most schools have accepted these costs as necessary and incorporated them into their budget process. However, when budget cuts are required, computing and telecommunications expenses are likely to be trimmed well before others (especially salaries). Similarly, the costs of having a computer and ongoing ISP charges have been accepted by most students and their parents as essential to schooling (along with books and supplies)—assuming that they can afford it. So, these types of costs have largely been assimilated by educational institutions and families, provided they fall into the category of "haves" rather than "have-nots."

A major economic consequence of online education is that it has created new market opportunities for computer and telecommunication companies,

The National Center for Technology Planning (http://www.nctp.com), created by Larry Anderson, is a useful resource for technology planning information.

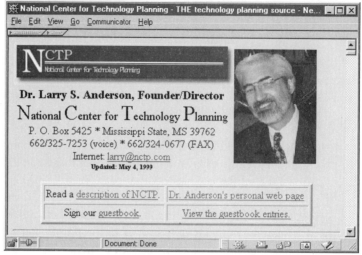

not just in hardware or software but in services as well (see C. Martin, 1999; Tapscott, 1997). The Web has spawned a tremendous range of new educational ventures, from course delivery tools to test preparation companies. Perhaps the most interesting new entities are the many for-profit "virtual schools." At the present time, these organizations are not much more than online versions of the classic "home study" companies. However, this is likely to change in the near future.

Virtual Schools

For the past hundred years, the model for educational offerings has been well defined: public or private schools catering to either the K–12 or post-secondary level. The only new development during this time has been the emergence of preschools, mostly private but some operated by churches and corporations. A small number of companies have offered "home study" courses on specialized subjects, and professional/trade associations have provided courses of relevance to their membership.

Online education permits new forms of institutions to evolve from those that currently exist or to develop from scratch (see Davidow & Malone, 1992; Hazemi, Hailes, & Wilbur, 1998; Rossman, 1992). For example, there is no reason why a group of experts in a given subject area can't start their own online "institute," offering courses or seminars and even conferring degrees or certificates. To be meaningful, such a virtual school would want to be ac-

Ziff-Davis University (ZDU) is a virtual school created by a media company (http://www.zdu.com). Tuition is a small monthly cost.

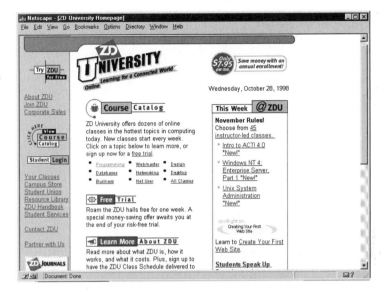

credited and would need to go through the accreditation process. Although accreditation as it currently exists is intended for large institutions, it could be changed to fit smaller entities. If a virtual school offered courses on topics in high demand (such as new areas of science, medicine, or technology) from very credible teachers, it could be quite successful.

Another possibility for virtual schools is that large publishing or media corporations may begin to offer online courses. Such organizations possess substantial libraries of suitable course materials that they already sell to students and schools. In the current model, teachers create and offer courses around these materials within the context of their institutions. But suppose that instructors developed and delivered their courses through media/publishing companies directly to students. If these companies became accredited, they could award credits and confer degrees. Or they could sell courses (along with the teachers) to existing institutions for them to offer. This idea is basically an extension of the traditional author/publisher model, except that it includes delivery of the course as well as its creation. Of course, many such efforts would involve teams, including company staff and freelance consultants.

Finally, we should allow for existing institutions or organizations to spin off groups or transform themselves entirely to create virtual schools. Because the financial resources required to start a virtual school are very small (the cost of the computing equipment, software, and telecommunications), and the potential revenue of worldwide student audiences very large, many people will find this a tempting opportunity. Indeed, virtual schools represent the educational gold rush of the information age.

Organizations That Shape Online Education

Many organizations shape current and future developments in the field of online computing. They include technology companies that develop hardware and software products that enable new networking capabilities. They also includes research and development (R&D) centers, as well as the funding agencies and foundations that make it possible for R&D to be conducted. Finally, certain schools, associations, and companies can strongly influence the direction of online computing by the nature of their projects, programs, or products. In this section, we highlight nine organizations (in no particular order) that stand out in terms of their contributions.

The Association for the Advancement of Computing in Education (AACE) provides conferences and publications for teachers about online education (http://www.aace.org).

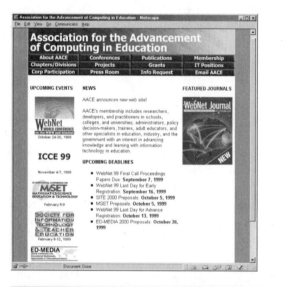

Technical Education Research Center (TERC) has been conducting research projects that focus on the use of technology in math and science education since 1965. In recent years, TERC (http://www.terc.edu) has spearheaded a number of major online projects, including Kids Network (in conjunction with the National Geographic Society) and GlobalLab.

Though not specifically concerned with education or networking, the MIT Media Lab (http://www.media.mit.edu) has developed demonstration projects and prototypes that strongly influence the entire technology world, especially in terms of multimedia capabilities.

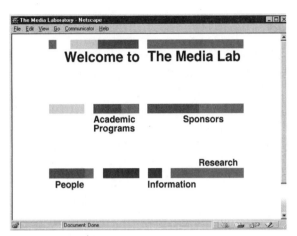

While many government agencies have done an excellent job providing online access to their resources, NASA (http://www.nasa.gov) has been a leader in terms of working with schools and creating worthwhile learning programs. It also helps that their subject matter is exciting and fascinating to kids and adults alike.

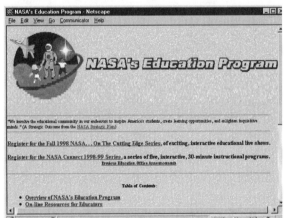

Although many telecommunications companies have become heavily involved in school networking, Pacific Bell was one of the first to provide substantial funds ($100 million) and broad support for online education with its Education First initiative and Knowledge Network Web site (http://www.kn.pacbell.com).

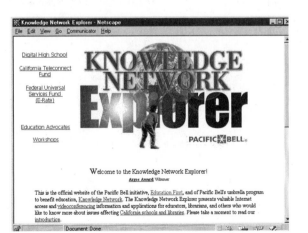

The British Open University (http://www.open.ac.uk) not only is the world's largest and most successful distance learning institution, but also makes extensive use of online education. The OU also hosts a number of advanced research groups such as the Knowledge Media Institute.

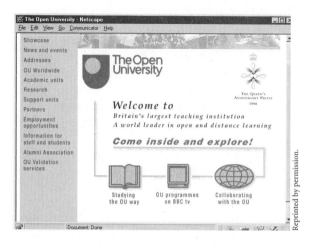

The National Center for Supercomputer Applications (NCSA) at the University of Illinois (http://www.ncsa.uiuc.edu) is one of the nation's leading research centers for high-performance computing and networking. This is where the original Web browser (Mosaic) was developed.

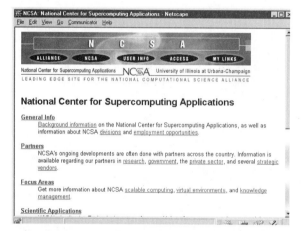

Though not as large as some other computer companies, Hewlett-Packard (http://www.hp.com) has always exerted a significant impact on the evolution of computing and its development in education (especially on the West Coast). Their Educator's Corner site, shown here, allows engineering students to use virtual test and measurement equipment.

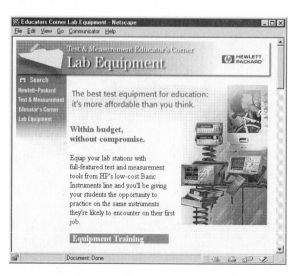

The National Institutes of Health (NIH) has been a leader in providing online access to medical information, beginning with its Medline database in the 1960s. Their Office of Science Education site, shown here, provides curriculum support materials for high school science (http://science-education.nih.gov).

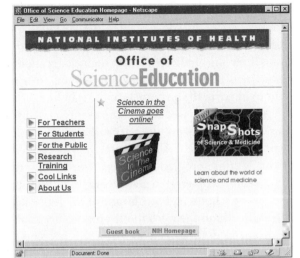

Resistance to Change

Because technology entails major changes in the way education is designed and delivered, it creates a great deal of resistance among individuals and organizations (Cuban, 1986; Feenberg, 1991). The reasons for resistance to change are varied: fear of the unknown, additional effort required to learn new things, loss of power/prestige due to changed roles, disagreement about new ideas. Because online learning/teaching is so different from traditional classroom instruction, it is very likely that some faculty, students, and administrators will object strongly (see, for example, "Digital Diploma Mills" by David Noble at http://firstmonday.dk/issues/issue3_1/noble/index.html).

Such objections can be addressed in a variety of ways. One is to ensure that on-campus classes are offered for those who don't want to learn/teach online. (However, this may not be a viable option in the future.) Another is to ensure that faculty and staff are involved in the design of online courses so that they develop some ownership of the effort. Student discomfort with the idea of online learning may be reduced by listening to other students who have taken online courses and been happy with them (perhaps on videotape). The same strategy can be used for faculty.

It is always necessary to "sell" people on the benefits of innovations in order to get them to try something new. In the case of online education, the primary benefit to students and faculty is flexibility in the time and location of learning/teaching. Not having to make the trip to campus for classes is a big selling factor for most people. Most teachers are intrigued by the opportunity to teach more effectively, or at least in new and different ways. For administrators (and some faculty), the capability to reach new student populations, and hence increase or maintain course enrollments, is important. And almost everyone understands that online education plugs them into the information age, although this may not be much of a motivation for those who want to linger in the quaintness of the traditional classroom.

Although online education represents a real paradigm shift in education, it will take place by evolutionary rather than revolutionary change. In every institution, a few courses at a time will be converted to online form, until gradually entire programs and departments go virtual. There will be the impatient early adopters, the mainstream middle group, and the reluctant holdouts. Some schools and organizations will move faster or slower than others, depending upon their economic and political milieu. But at some point in the 21st century, online education will become the norm and traditional classroom instruction will be an anachronism.

Conclusion

Online education seems to be a relatively positive development for learning and teaching, although it certainly raises some questions about how it might affect individuals, organizations, and society overall. It should open up new opportunities for students and teachers as well as educational institutions. But it might have adverse consequences for some which can't be foreseen at this juncture. It is clear that online education will impact access to education, the economics of learning, privacy, and the nature of schools. There is no doubt that the information age is an exciting time to be a student, a teacher, an administrator, or an educational entrepreneur.

Curtis Bonk: Electronic Collaboration

Curtis Bonk is an associate professor in the School of Education at the University of Indiana and a member of the Center for Research on Learning and Technology. He is the developer of "smartweb," an online environment for mentoring undergraduate educational psychology students as well as other tools for Web-based learning. He is coeditor of the book *Electronic Collaborators: Learner-centered Technologies for Literacy, Apprenticeship, and Discourse*, published in 1998 by Erlbaum. He has recently proposed a ten-level model for online learning.

To learn more about his work, see http://php.indiana.edu/~cjbonk.

Key Ideas

- The most significant issue in online education is accessibility: Does it widen the gap between the haves and the have-nots?
- Is network technology inherently good? Might online education have some serious drawbacks for certain individuals or society overall?
- Are educational institutions taking appropriate steps to ensure the privacy of online learners?
- Is online education affordable and cost-effective?
- Virtual schools open up new opportunities for existing institutions as well as for new kinds of educational organizations.
- Online education generates considerable resistance to change.

Questions for Further Reflection

1. Does technology reduce or increase the gap between the haves and the have-nots?
2. Is technology inherently neutral?
3. How serious are concerns about privacy in online education?
4. Will online learning raise or lower the costs of education (or neither)?
5. Will virtual schools improve or diminish the quality of education?
6. What do you think is the best way to deal with resistance to change?

11

When the Electrons Hit the Screen

After completing this chapter, you should understand

- factors to take into account in developing an online course

- some of the practical issues associated with online education, including getting connected, selecting software, and troubleshooting

Cyberspace has become a globe-girdling amplifier for human touch, a vehicle for linking people around the globe into new kinds of communities that transcend time and space. (Smolan & Erwitt, 1996, p. 19)

Previous chapters have addressed major conceptual issues in online education. In this chapter, we consider a variety of practical concerns that arise during the implementation of online courses. Such concerns include putting together an online class, getting connected, finding money and resources, selecting software, troubleshooting, and deciding what to do next. Most of these concerns build upon the issues introduced in earlier chapters.

Putting Together an Online Course

Many instructors, schools, and organizations are just getting started with online education. In Chapter 7, we discussed some of the issues associated with the design and development of online courses. There are also quite a number of practical considerations that need to be addressed.

First, it is a lot easier to convert an existing class into online form than to develop something brand new. With a new course, both the curriculum (content) and the delivery format (online teaching/learning) have to be debugged simultaneously. If the course has been taught for a while and seems to be working, then it is possible to concentrate on the changes associated with the new delivery format. At the same time, putting an existing course in online format will normally require some significant changes to the way the course is taught and the content. In light of the discussion presented in Chapter 6 about interactivity and student participation, as well as the engagement model outlined in Chapter 5, the learning activities in an online course are likely to be quite different from those in the typical classroom version.

Indeed, the starting point for creating an online course (beyond goals/objectives) is the definition of student assignments/exercises. The nature of the assignments will determine the level of interactivity and participation in a course. For example, asking students to post their responses to a question in a discussion forum ensures a certain level of interaction (reading each other's responses). Having students upload a report to the instructor and giving them individual feedback messages about their work represents another type of interactivity. And directing students to take an online quiz or test that provides them with their score and feedback about correct/incorrect choices provides yet another kind of interaction. The form of the assignments will depend on the learning goals/objectives of the course and what kinds of online learning tools are available.

Many colleges and universities have excellent faculty development programs that provide support for development of online courses. An example is the Hawaii Community College system (http://www.hcc.hawaii. edu/intranet/committees/FacDevCom/index.htm).

Another decision to be made is the extent to which students will work individually or in groups. Students may work together on major projects but do weekly assignments by themselves. Or all assignments may be done collaboratively, either with the same partners or in different groups each week. Whenever students are working collaboratively, a methodology is needed for defining group composition—whether random, self-chosen, or based on commonalties. Groups may have a designated leader, be leaderless, or have defined roles. Since many students lack experience working in groups, they will often need considerable guidance in how to function effectively in a team environment. Unless such procedures are defined by the software (groupware programs), it will be up to the instructor to define and explain all the parameters of group interaction.

Once these decisions about the nature of interactivity and student participation have been made, it is time to develop the course documents described in Chapter 7: syllabus, lesson plan, and study guide. The exact nature of the course will depend largely on the course tools available and the online environment to be used. The development process will be shaped by the team members involved—their design skills and experience with online education.

The most difficult aspect of creating an online course for many instructors is dealing with their propensity to lecture. Changing their role from pre-

The Tech-Learning site (http://www.techlearning.com) is a source for online teaching ideas as well as software reviews.

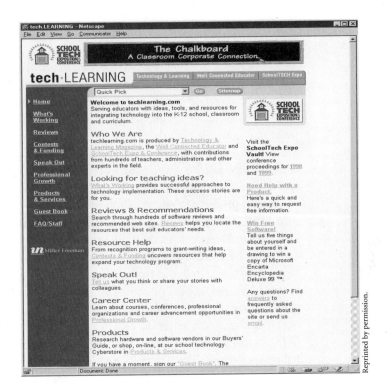

Reprinted by permission.

senter to facilitator or moderator is not easy to accept. If an online course is designed to follow the engagement model outlined in Chapter 5 and includes a decent syllabus and study guide, there should be little need for instructor presentations. Nonetheless, many instructors still feel the need to provide lectures via digital audio/video segments or real-time conferencing. Although such lectures may enhance the instructional effectiveness of the course (or at least make it more interesting), they also can distract attention from learning activities that involve student interaction and participation—which should be the primary function of an online instructor.

One last piece of advice about creating a first course is to begin with a pilot or prototype. Before a lot of effort is expended in the design and development of the full course, make up a sample lesson or two and try it out with a small number of representative students. Such a pilot study can identify any major problems with the design and avoid wasted time/effort. Ideally, the full version of the course will also be tried out with a small group of students before offering it as an actual class, so that small problems can be discovered and fixed. Conducting pilot testing is an important aspect of the quality control measures discussed in Chapter 9.

Getting Connected

As has been mentioned many times earlier in this book, online education only works if everyone involved (students, faculty, and administrative staff) has regular access to computers and networks. The extent to which this condition is satisfied varies considerably across individuals and institutions. In general, most postsecondary students and employees of large organizations meet it, whereas those in school settings and small organizations do not. Other complications associated with socioeconomic standing, culture, and special needs have been discussed in Chapters 5 and 10.

Access problems need to be solved at two basic levels: individuals and institutional. At the individual level, students and employees need to have their own personal network accounts as provided by an ISP. Such an account carries a cost of at least $20 per month, depending on the kind of connection. Many people try to avoid this expense by relying on institutional accounts provided by their school or company. Although an institutional account may suffice, it has a number of disadvantages, including lack of personal control over files and access, potential reliability problems, and lack of transferability. Individuals and families should consider the monthly ISP fee to be an essential utility expense like electricity or telephone. Providers of online education should expect students to have an ISP connection as a prerequisite to taking any online courses.

Having suitable hardware and software to access networks is much less of a concern today than in earlier times. Most computers today include a built-in modem and the operating system includes a browser with email capability. Configuring the hardware and software with the particular network IDs and passwords can be a challenge, although no more so than setting up any other application (and falls under the category of basic computer literacy as discussed in Chapter 5). If the connection involves a LAN, broadband, or multimedia (such as desktop video) capability, it will be more complicated and may require technical assistance. Such assistance should be available from the ISP, vendors of the products being used, or the institution that is being connected to. Installing new versions of network software, or learning new kinds of network applications, is an ongoing chore that every network user must accept.

Getting connected at the institutional level is a much more complex endeavor. The kind of network connection appropriate for a given school or organization depends on its size (number of students/employees/customers) and the nature of the online applications. For example, an engineering or medical school that is providing very computationally intensive programs (such as simulations or data analysis tools) will require a lot of bandwidth

All technology vendors offer online support for their products—for example, Sun Microsystems (http://www.sun.com/service/online). These vendor sites can be a useful resource when trouble-shooting network problems.

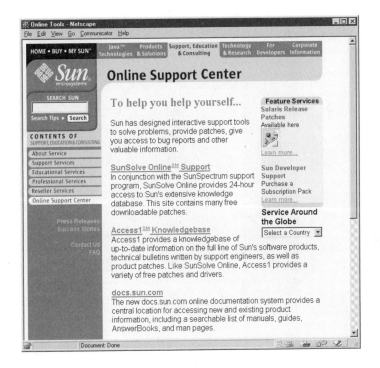

and very powerful servers. However, a high school that is primarily support-ing email and discussion forums for its classes will not need a great deal of bandwidth or server capability. The addition of LANs to the network or any form of multimedia computing (such as streaming, audio/video, or video-conferencing) will require significantly more bandwidth and computing power.

Determining exactly what hardware, software, and telecommunications equipment an institution needs requires considerable technical expertise. Large organizations and school systems will have staff dedicated to this task—not only installing networks initially, but also maintaining and up-grading them. (One thing that can be said with certainty about networks is that they will need maintaining and upgrading.) In smaller companies and schools, vendors will probably provide network support, or consultants will supply assistance as needed. In some cases, teaching staff and students will be drafted into service to provide network support if they have the necessary technical background or training.

Most institutions have a technology plan that attempts to describe cur-rent and projected network needs. Data on computing applications and net-work usage are collected periodically from the user population. Network

Many states have created extensive online resources for their school systems, including information about training and funding for technology. An example is the Link 2 Learn network in Pennsylvania (http://l2l.org/index.html).

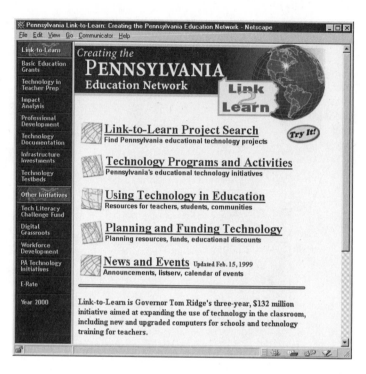

planners also need to monitor new technology developments (see the next chapter) as well as study what other institutions are doing. Forecasting network needs is a difficult task but an essential one, because it usually takes long time periods (one to two years) to implement new network capabilities. Well-run organization are able to provide additional network capabilities in a timely fashion because they have anticipated needs and put new capabilities in place in advance of their actual use.

Finding Money and Resources

In the preceding chapter, we discussed briefly the costs and benefits of online education. Finding the money and resources (facilities, staff) to implement and maintain networks is a major problem for every educational administrator or manager. Networks seem to be a financial vortex, sucking up money and resources as fast as they can be made available. The reason is that network capabilities are unbounded and can expand as fast as people become aware of them.

Most institutions and organizations recognize network costs as a regular budget item and plan accordingly. However, many schools find it difficult to

The Pitsco Web site (http://www.pitsco.com) includes a very comprehensive guide to funding resources as well as information about many of the topics covered in earlier chapters. It also hosts the "Ask an Expert" page—a unique resource for students.

Reprinted by permission.

squeeze any more money out of their existing budgets for technology (or anything else) and require external assistance in the form of grants or donations. Some schools have established partnerships with technology or telecommunications vendors that donate equipment and support services. Other schools have reached out for state or federal money, or in the case of colleges and universities, private donations.

In Chapter 8, we discussed some of the facilities and staffing considerations associated with networks. Facilities tend to be the least significant problem because network equipment does not usually require much room. However, when the facilities needed include computer labs or electronic classrooms, they become more of a concern. In most cases, existing classrooms are overhauled for computer use—something that can be done relatively inexpensively or quite lavishly, depending on the political motivations associated with the use of technology. For example, at a major university, one electronic classroom was created at a modest cost using standard furniture and computer systems while another was created with custom-made furniture, computers, and fixtures for an enormous amount of money. The latter was funded by a private donation, whereas the former used regular budget funds.

Staffing is typically the biggest network problem for most schools and educational organizations. Most colleges rely on their own students (especially graduate students in engineering and computer science) for network support. Schools tend to make as much use as they can of teachers with technical backgrounds; larger school systems usually have a limited number of technical staff that are shared across the system. Many schools and small organizations make extensive use of consultants and vendors to provide network support, which avoids the need for salaried positions. Large organizations tend to have their own network support staff as part of their Information Technology departments. However, even when the money is available to hire such staff, it is often difficult to find properly qualified individuals and/or keep them up to date on technology. Ironically, this is one area where online education can made a major contribution: the training and retraining of network support personnel. All of the network technology companies (for example, Microsoft, Cisco, IBM) provide online training in their products.

To a large extent, the success of administrators and managers in finding money to fund their network activities will affect the viability of their institutions and organizations. As online education becomes a larger part of all educational offerings, such funding will become one of the major financial concerns of educators in the 21st century.

Selecting Software

Software selection is a decision process that goes on at all levels of online education. Students need to make decisions about what application and browser software they will use (although Microsoft tries to keep the options limited to their products). Instructors and course developers make decisions about which online applications and authoring environments they will use (Chapters 3 and 7). Network administrations make decisions about what online environments will be implemented and supported, as well as the server and telecommunications software to be used. All of these software decisions have financial and instructional implications.

The costs of software tend to be borne by institutions and not students. For example, when a school provides courses using an online environment such as WebCT or Lotus Learning Space, it pays a license fee for use by its students. Similarly, the costs of server software are paid for by the institution. Students don't even have to pay for their applications or browser software because this is usually bundled with the computer system they buy. More advanced programs, such as multimedia tools, are often available as free downloads, at least for a specified evaluation period. From a student's (and instructor's) perspective, the only real cost associated with software is the time required to learn how to use it; hence software tends to be valued in terms of its utility and usability.

Institutions tend to select software on the basis of licensing fees, dependability, and extent of support. Dependability and support are largely a function of longevity; that is, products that have been around the longest tend to be the most dependable and best supported. For example, many commercial products (such as Netscape and CuSeeMe) have their origins in public-domain programs developed in the university community, where they received extensive testing and use before becoming products. As a rule, the software selection process at most institutions is not particularly rational and is subject to the personal preferences (and sometimes whimsy) of key decision-makers. Large school systems tend to have formal evaluation criteria and a review process for making software purchases, although individual schools can often override these decisions. In postsecondary institutions, an advisory committee usually scrutinizes software decisions, but individual departments and faculty members have considerable autonomy.

There is also a strong "fad" element to network software selection. New programs develop communities of use across schools, which evangelize on

Product reviews can be useful in selecting software. One of many sources is the Benchin Web site (http:// www.benchin.com), which features user reviews.

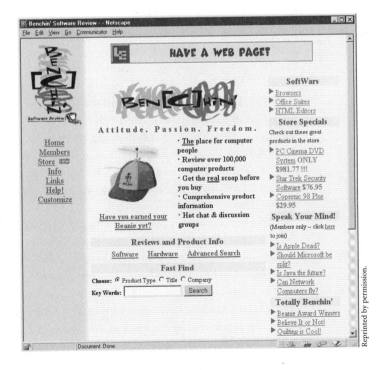

Reprinted by permission.

behalf of the programs. Given the power of networks to reach many individuals in a short time, it is not too surprising that such evangelists are able to promote their favorite software very effectively. Strong rivalries often develop between groups at different institutions supporting similar programs. However, once a program has caught on at enough institutions, it becomes rooted in the educational world and becomes well known and widely used. Such programs are not always the best of their class, but the ones that circumstances favored.

Probably the most frustrating aspect of software selection for all concerned is its short life span. It seems as though few network programs have a lifetime of more than a year or two between major revisions or obsolescence. Consequently, there is a constant need to upgrade or change software. A decision not to upgrade or change means you will be out of synch with everyone else and eventually will not be able to read files from others. The simplest way to deal with this dilemma is simply to replace your computer every few years, assuming that it comes with the latest software installed.

Troubleshooting

A general skill required by all computer users is troubleshooting—being able to figure why something isn't working and fix it. This skill is especially important for online activities, which tend to be fairly complicated applications. Modern network software, including browsers and learning environments, makes it relatively easy to accomplish tasks. But things do go wrong, and frequently.

Probably the most common problem that online users experience is failure to establish a network connection. There are many possible reasons: a network server or router is down, the phone line is disconnected or not operational, the system configuration has changed, or there is a modem problem. Whenever passwords are involved, problems are bound to occur because people forget or mistype them. Web URLs often change or are entered incorrectly.

Another common problem is with incorrect file types. People are unable to download or open a file because their software cannot read it. This happens commonly with file attachments to email because the settings in the email program are not configured for the type of file attached. Or the file was created using a different version (older or newer) of an application program than the one available on your computer. And graphic files are always dicey, given the number of different graphic formats. Luckily, programs such as Adobe Acrobat (PDF format) and RealMedia create standards for certain kinds of files.

Anyone who teaches online has to spend a considerable amount of time helping students troubleshoot their network problems. One way to minimize this time is to try to have all students use the same software. A major virtue of online learning environments that provide an integrated set of tools is that they decrease software variability among students and make troubleshooting easier. Another useful technique is to develop a FAQ page for problems that students can read if they have difficulties (assuming they can get online). Software vendors that provide free telephone or online support for their products also help to reduce the troubleshooting load of an instructor.

Not all problems encountered in online courses result from network software or computer systems; some come from mistakes or ambiguities in course materials (for example, wrong dates, bad links, missing content). Such mistakes should be discovered as part of quality control efforts (pilot testing, technical reviews), but these efforts are often lacking in educational settings. Although these problems usually have nothing specifically to do with the network aspects of a course, they tend to be perceived as deficiencies of online education. In any event, they need to be rectified by the course team.

Just as the development of an online course is normally a team effort, so is troubleshooting. While the instructor will bear the heaviest burden of

THE Journal Online (http://www.thejournal.com) not only contains articles about technology applications but also provides a roadmap to the Internet.

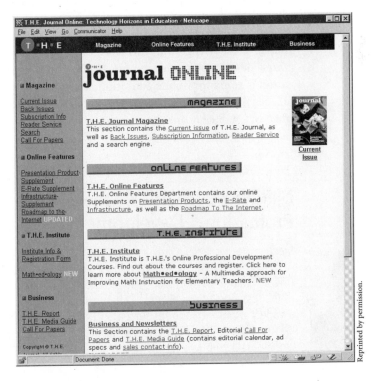

responsibility for problems, there needs to be a technical support person who can handle network difficulties and an administrative support person who takes care of administrative matters. Each of these individuals may serve as the interface to other kinds of support personnel within the institution (such as counseling, financial aid, student services, or computer help).

The importance of good troubleshooting procedures in online education cannot be overemphasized. Students (as well as faculty) are often isolated, with no local resources or support. They are dependent on the support provided remotely to address and solve their problems. If problems are not solved promptly, they impede learning progress and quickly wear down the motivation to continue learning. Ultimately, the troubleshooting effectiveness of a program will affect the success of its online courses.

Conclusion

This chapter has touched on only a few of the practical matters that educators will encounter as they implement online education. Anyone embarking on the design or delivery of an online course, whether a teacher, administrator, or instructional developer, should do a number of things: (1) Search the Web for existing online courses that involve similar content, students, tools, or objectives, and study them. (2) Talk to others in your institution or elsewhere who have done what you plan to do. (3) Take an online course if you have no firsthand experience with this form of learning. (4) Put together a team for course development and support. (5) Ensure that your institution or organization is ready for online education. The last will be difficult to determine if you are the first to try an online offering, but thinking through the issues outlined in Chapters 8 and 9 may help.

Mariano Bernardez: Online Professional Development

Mariano Bernardez is a well-known training consultant who lives in Buenos Aires, Argentina. In 1998, he founded the Performance Improvement Global Network (PIGN) chapter of the organization ISPI (http://www.pignc-ispi.com). PIGN is one of the first virtual (and bilingual) chapters of a professional association. It provides a variety of information resources and discussion opportunities to members of ISPI and the training community—as well as a nice demonstration of how networks can link up two continents.

One of the easiest ways to avail yourself of information and ideas about online education (apart from Web browsing) is to attend a conference of any organization devoted to educational technology (see Chapter 13) or education/training in a given domain. A conference provides an opportunity to learn from the experience of others, see demonstrations of software and systems, and gauge the current trends.

Key Ideas

- When first developing an online course, try to work from an existing offering, focusing on the nature of the assignments/exercises and group work.
- Providers of online courses need to ensure that network connections are available for both individuals and institutions.
- Network costs for equipment, facilities, and staff may require budget changes or special funding.
- Selection of network software is primarily an institutional problem; decisions are based on costs, capabilities, and extent of use.
- Online courses require ongoing troubleshooting efforts to run smoothly.

Questions for Further Reflection

1. Are there any advantages to choosing a completely new course for online delivery (rather than an existing one)?
2. If you were the first person to develop and offer an online course in your setting, what things should you be concerned about?
3. What do you think is the most difficult aspect of getting connected for new network users?
4. Do you think that funding for networks will always be a problem, or do you anticipate that this concern will fade in importance? Why?
5. In terms of selecting software, can you suggest some additional considerations that should be taken in account other than those mentioned?
6. What kinds of solutions would you propose for troubleshooting in online courses?

12

Future Directions

After completing this chapter, you should understand

- the likely direction of technology developments
- that nobody really has any idea where this is all going

Over the course of the industrial revolution, motors shrank in size and cost, disappearing inside household appliances and workplace tools to create new kinds of machines. Through a similar process, we are now embedding computers and telecommunications into our everyday context, making possible three innovative types of learning devices. Smart objects, with embedded microprocessors and wireless networking, explain their own functioning and help us create "articulate" educational environments that communicate with their inhabitants. Information infrastructures provide remote access to experts, interlinked archival resources, virtual communities, and "distributed" investigations involving many participants in different locations. Shared synthetic environments, by immersing us in illusion, help us develop a better understanding and appreciation of reality. The new messages emerging from these new media can dramatically improve instructional outcomes, but such an evolution of educational practice depends on careful design of the interface among the devices, learners, and teachers. (Dede, 1996)

So far in this book we have examined online education as it is today. But there are many interesting possibilities for how networks might be used in the future. This chapter considers some of these potential applications. Of course, trying to predict the future is folly and must be viewed as a purely speculative exercise; however, the opening quote from Chris Dede (a futurist by training) provides some good conjectures.

Ubiquitous Computing

One technology development that seems easy to predict is the increasing prevalence of microprocessors in all objects—making them "smart." We have become used to having computers in devices like cars and coffeemakers, but many believe this is just the beginning. For example, it is predicted that we will have computers embedded in clothes and jewelry, as well as furniture and furnishings. The purpose of such microprocessors will be to process data for personal preferences, security/safety, or networking. It will not be necessary to have a computer at hand in order to receive email messages or find information; your shirt or sofa may be able to perform these functions. Of course, these kinds applications are predicated on speech input/output for human–computer interaction, something that has been long anticipated but slow to materialize.

Xerox Palo Alto Research Center (PARC), one of the most influential R&D labs in the computing field, has made significant contributions to the nature of personal computers and networking (http://www.parc.xerox.com).

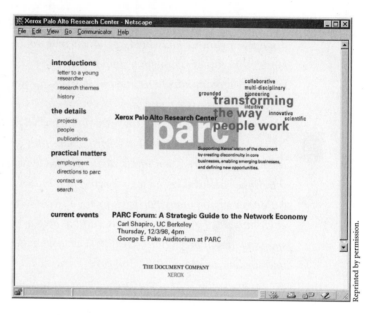

A key element of ubiquitous computing is wireless networking. We already have simple forms of wireless networking—the use of infrared connections in LAN settings and radio frequency (cellular) in WANs. However, current forms of wireless networks are less dependable and more expensive than direct (wired) connection. With the advent of satellite-based cellular services, this is likely to change for the WAN environment. But the kind of ubiquitous computing envisioned by many will require much more robust forms of wireless networking than are available now.

What is the significance of ubiquitous computing for education? It should mean that online learning activities can be conducted in a much broader and more natural range of learning settings, because it will not be necessary to have students seated at computers in labs or at desks. It may also reduce the "haves/have-nots" dilemma because computing capability would be everywhere and not restricted to the well-off. Perhaps having smarter devices around will make it easier for students and teachers to use computer resources for learning.

Intelligent Software

Correlated with the emergence of ubiquitous computing is the development of intelligent software—programs capable of making autonomous decisions based on the input received or what they sense about the state of the environ-

The Research Division of IBM Corporation (http://www.research.ibm.com) is another very influential R&D lab in the computing world, especially in terms of new hardware developments.

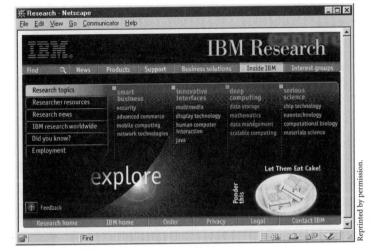

Reprinted by permission.

ment. In the case of ubiquitous computing, these decisions are most likely to involve personal preferences or routine procedures, such as turning on lights and setting them to appropriate levels or logging on to a network and checking email automatically when you enter your office. Although such actions are relatively mundane, they represent small decisions that people don't have to be bothered with and are relatively easy and safe for computers to carry out.

A lot of intelligent software will probably take the form of "agents"—programs that are capable of performing a specialized task such as formulating an email message, conducting a regular search of a database, or setting up a spreadsheet for a particular type of analysis. In fact, many applications such as word processing and slide show programs already include agents (called "wizards") that automatically take care of formatting or layout decisions. However, a more powerful class of agent programs will have enough understanding of their domain (as well as human nature) to be able to perform tasks that at present require more complex decision making. It is also likely that agents will be driven by speech input, enabling computers to recognize and carry out verbal commands—for example, "Send an email message to my husband and tell him that I will be late for dinner."

In the instructional domain, efforts to develop intelligent software for teaching have been going on for many years under the name "intelligent tutoring systems" (for example, Farr & Psotka, 1992; Poulson & Richardson, 1988). The idea behind intelligent tutoring systems was to create programs that understood enough about a particular subject or task domain to be able to answer student questions and grade assignments—in essence, simulate an expert teacher. However, intelligent tutoring systems turned out to be

Bell Labs, a component of Lucent Technologies, is the premier R&D lab for new developments in telecommunications technology (http://www.bell-labs.com).

prohibitively expensive and time-consuming to develop and consequently have had no practical applications so far. Perhaps at some point in the future this approach may be more viable—although the development of intelligent agents for programs used in educational applications seems more likely to be worthwhile.

Merging of Television, Telecommunications, and Computing

A long predicted development that is just now beginning to materialize is the merging of the television, telecommunications, and computing worlds. This development is most clearly demonstrated by Web-TV—the ability to access the Web, via a specially equipped television, through the services of television cable/satellite providers. Moving television content, such as movies, home shopping, or talk shows, to the Web (using digital video) is the commercial force underlying this development. Media companies believe they can make more money if they can deliver personalized content to homes, especially in an interactive context where orders can be placed or people can participate actively in programming.

The implications of this development for education are already apparent. Television networks (such as CNN and Discovery) have created Web sites that provide curriculum or teacher materials to support their programming—hoping that such value-added materials will make their broadcasting more useful (and used) in the classroom. Once the bandwidth is available to provide video online, there is little doubt that networks will package and market their programming directly to schools, students, and parents. This marketing will be no different from what book publishers have done for years, except that the content will be more dynamic and attention-grabbing than print materials.

·This merging of the telecommunications and computer industries should also make real-time conferencing (especially videoconferencing) a more viable form of interaction, particularly if digital televisions can be used as the conferencing device. If the cost becomes reasonable (equivalent to a phone call) and the quality of the video is good (at least 30 frames/second), people are likely to use conferencing a lot. This would enhance student and teacher interaction in online courses as well as make remote guest participation easier and more interesting.

Virtual Environments

In Chapter 3, we briefly discussed the value of simulation as an instructional methodology. An even more worthwhile version of simulation is virtual reality—which is basically 3-D simulation with sensorimotor input and output. In a virtual environment, students have realistic learning experiences that include the ability to manipulate objects or navigate around 3-D representations of actual or imagined worlds. Obvious applications for virtual reality are science or medical labs that involve working with simulated equipment or biological entities. More intriguing are virtual worlds for mathematics, astronomy, or geology that involve visual representations of abstract concepts. It is also likely that virtual reality will be used extensively for the humanities and fine arts, where it can extend traditional modalities of expression.

Virtual reality can also be used for interpersonal interaction to create shared synthetic environments. This is the 3-D equivalent of the MUDs/MOOs discussed in Chapter 3. Instead of being limited to typed descriptions of other individuals, people can see and touch 3-D representations called "avatars." In theory, individuals could conduct any kind of team or group activity in a virtual reality environment that they would do in reality, except that the virtual environment does not have to adhere to the laws of physics or biology. So, students could go on space exploration adventures, journeys through the body, or trips back in time. Indeed, we can expect virtual reality technology to show up at Disney World long before it appears in classrooms!

The Virtual Reality Lab at the University of Michigan (http://www-VRL.umich.edu) is one of a number of R&D facilities around the world that are exploring this technology.

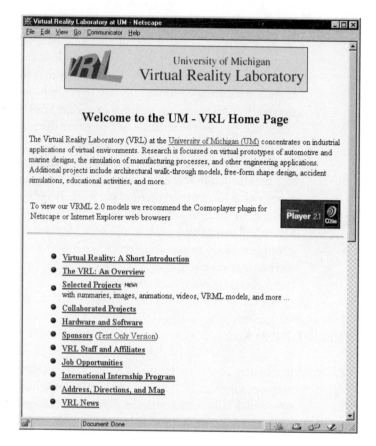

Unfortunately, creating virtual reality environments is a very expensive and time-consuming process, which will limit educational applications. However, we can expect to see it used in the training world (especially airline and military training). The application of virtual reality to science education is demonstrated by the Science Space project (http://www.virtual.gwu.edu). For more discussion about virtual reality and its application in schools, see the VR & Schools newsletter at http://eastnet.educ.ecu.edu/vr/pub.htm.

Speech Processing

One of assumptions made by many science fiction writers and those who write future computing scenarios is that people will interact with computers primarily via speech. Speech input and output is seen as a more natural form of interaction than the use of keyboards and mice. Since it allows "hands-free" interaction, it fits in with ubiquitous computing devices that might be worn as jewelry (the proverbial "Dick Tracy" wristwatch) or embedded in furniture/furnishings.

Even though speech input and output capabilities have been around in one form or another for many years, they have been slow to catch on. Part of the reason is that existing speech processing capabilities have been rather limited, with difficult-to-understand synthesized speech and speech recognition that can handle only a small number of isolated words. It is reasonable to expect that with better-quality speech synthesis and recognition, people might use it more frequently. Another problem, however, is that speech input does not allow for private interaction with the computer, which can be a problem in an office setting or classroom lab. Perhaps as people become more comfortable using voice input and output in the context of online conferences (and hence become used to wearing headsets), there will be more acceptance for speech processing.

Speech processing does have many potential educational benefits. Language learning programs have made good use of existing synthesis/recognition capabilities to allow students to listen to and practice pronunciations. Speech input and output are also very useful for young children learning to speak and read. In certain training settings, such as air traffic control or emergency services, speech processing capabilities are an important part of simulations. And text-to-speech conversion programs are a critical component for blind computer users. Many educational applications would probably be enhanced by the use of speech input/output.

To learn more about speech technology and research, see the Speech site at Carnegie-Mellon University (http://www.speech.cs.cmu.edu/speech), which also provides links to many other relevant sites.

Automated Language Translation

One of the exciting aspects of global networking is that it allows people from all nations to interact easily. This is especially true in the case of online education, where courses can involve participates from anywhere in the world. However, people speak different languages, which makes communication difficult. This problem is likely to get worse as more people get online.

The ideal solution is automatic translation programs that convert text from one language to another. Such software exists for many languages and is used by translators. But current translation software tends to be expensive and not sophisticated enough to be used by people unfamiliar with the languages involved. Demand for this capability is increasing, however, and translation software is getting better. Ideally, such programs would be

The AltaVista system (http://www.altavista.com) provides an automated translation capability.

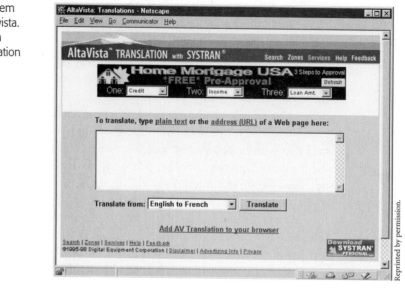

utilities built into email and word processing software so they can be used as needed.

The widespread availability of good language translation software would have an interesting effect on cross-cultural understanding and geopolitics. With the language barrier removed, people could easily read newspapers, government documents, and scholarly literature from other countries (assuming it's online). And there would be less opportunity for the censorship that takes place when documents are translated by "official sources." An interesting question is whether the availability of translation software would contribute to the preservation or homogenization of different cultures.

Knowledge Management

One of the most important developments in the training domain in the past decade has been the emphasis on organizational rather than individual learning (see Marquardt & Kearsley, 1999). The idea underlying organizational learning is to foster the sharing and accumulation of knowledge within an organization by capturing the expertise of employees and putting it in a form that is easily available to everyone else (present and future) who wants to access it. This type of information sharing is most easily accomplished via computer databases and networks. The creation of such databases and networks has come to be called knowledge management.

Major consulting firms such as Andersen Consulting (http://www.ac.com) are good sources of information about emerging technology and its impact on business.

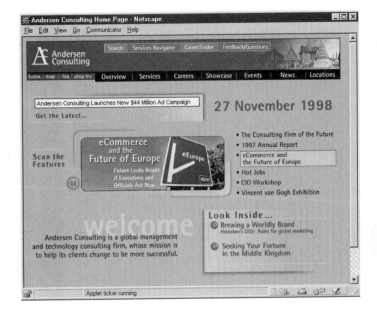

Knowledge management systems can be created for any aspect of an organization's operations. For example, a system might be established for sales and marketing that captures all the techniques and strategies used by salespeople in a company—including extensive details on customers.

Though not specifically concerned with technology, the Institute for the Future (http://www.iftf.org) is a well-known "think tank" that makes forecasts about emerging trends and developments in society.

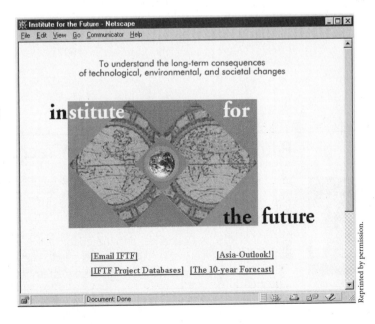

Alternatively, a system might be created for product maintenance and troubleshooting that identifies all the known problems and repair techniques associated with a company's products, based on the experiences of service technicians. Or a system might be developed for management that documents good (and bad) decision-making strategies, based on the behavior of past managers.

Although knowledge management systems have evolved in the corporate domain, there is no reason why they could not also be developed by educational institutions. Indeed, any large university or school system is tantamount to a major corporation, with the same kinds of business concerns (albeit not profit-making). Capturing and sharing the knowledge of experienced employees (including teachers) is something that educational institutions are interested in—hence they are good candidates for knowledge management systems as well.

A good source for further information about knowledge management is the Biz Tech Web site (http://www.brint.com).

Conclusion

This chapter has mentioned some developments in the field of computing that are likely to impact the future of online education. Whether these particular developments or others actually materialize, one thing can be said for certain: The 21st century will bring tremendous advances in computers and networks, dramatically changing our daily lives—and how we learn or teach.

For further discussion about future trends in technology, see Dertouzos (1997), Negroponte (1995), or Stefik (1997).

Paul Levinson: Information Technology Visionary

Paul Levinson is the founder and president of Connected Education Inc., an organization that has provided online courses in conjunction with major universities since 1985. He is the author of many books and articles about electronic communications, including *Digital McLuhan: A Guide to the Information Millennium* published in 1999 by Routledge, and the editor of the *Journal of Social and Evolutionary Systems*. Levinson is also a noted science fiction writer.

To learn more, see http://www.sfwa.org/members/Levinson.

Key
Ideas

- Ubiquitous computing will improve the accessibility of technology.
- Intelligent software will make technology easier to use.
- The merging of television, telecommunications, and computing will increase the information capabilities of online networks.
- Virtual reality will provide new forms of online interaction.
- Speech processing will make online interaction more natural.
- Automatic language translation will reduce cultural barriers and enhance international collaboration in online education.
- Knowledge management systems will allow us to capture experience and wisdom in online systems.

Questions for Further Reflection

1. Can you think of an example of ubiquitous computing that would make your life more comfortable or enjoyable?
2. What applications can you think of (educational or otherwise) for intelligent agents?
3. Describe a learning or teaching application that you think would be good for virtual reality.
4. What learning or teaching application would be improved by speech processing?
5. How would you use automated language translation capability?
6. What value would a knowledge management system have in your educational institution?

13 Sources of Further Information

After completing this chapter, you should understand

- where to find more information about online education

The compelling theme of my experience in cyberspace is that even though it may seem to a casual onlooker to be a dull technological experience, it is instead an intensely human experience. The transfer of bits across wires or waves is merely the technological means to the ultimate end of cyberspace communication—the sharing of human concerns, human ideas, human ideals, and human passions. That's the cyberspace I know—a human dimension of unlimited potential to bless or curse our lives. (Whittle, 1997, p. 412)

Although the preceding chapters of this book have laid out the basic characteristics of online education, they have barely scratched the surface. To really understand the depth and complexity of the subject, you need to get online and explore. Here are some ideas about where to start.

Journals/Magazines

The Wellspring: an online community of distance educators (http://wellspring.isinj.com)

CMC Magazine (http://www.december.com/cmc/mag/current/toc.html)

Educational Technology & Society (http://ifets.gmd.de/periodical)

Electronic Schools (http://www.electronic-school.com)

Networking: Online newsletter of the NODE program (http://node.on.ca/networking)

From Now On (http://fromnowon.org)

Journal of Asynchronous Learning Networks (http://www.aln.org/alnweb)

Journal of Interactive Multimedia in Education (http://www-jime.open.ac.uk)

Journal of Interactive Learning Research (http://www.aace.org)

Journal of Instructional Science & Technology (http://www.usq.edu.au/electpub/e-jist/homepage.htm)

Journal of Technology Education (http://scholar.lib.vt.edu/ejournals/JTE/jte.html)

New Horizons for Learning (http://www.newhorizons.org)

Online Educator (http://www.learnersonline.com)

On the Horizon (http://horizon.unc.edu)

Tech Learning (http://www.techlearning.com)

THE Journal (http://www.thejournal.com)

Multimedia Schools (http://www.infotoday.com/MMschools/default.htm)

First Monday (http://firstmonday.com)

New Chalk (http://www.unc.edu/courses/newchalk.html)

Syllabus (http://www.syllabus.com/syllmag.html)

Conference/Workshop Proceedings

AusWeb 97 (http://ausweb.scu.edu.au/ausweb97.htm)

NAU Web 98 (http://star.ucc.nau.edu/~nauweb98)

NSF Future of Networking Technologies for Learning (http://www.ed.gov/
Technology/Futures)

Teaching at Community Colleges Online (http://leahi.kcc.hawaii.edu/org/
tcon98/papers.html)

Associations

American Association of School Administrators (http://www.aasa.org)

American Education Research Association (http://aera.net)

American Society for Training & Development (http://www.astd.org)

Association for the Advancement of Computers in Education (http://
www.aace.org)

Association for Educational Communication and Technology (http://
www.aect.org)

Association for Supervision and Curriculum Development (http://
www.ascd.org)

Computer Using Educators (http://www.cue.org)

Distance Education Training Council (http://www.detc.org)

EduCause (http://www.educause.edu)

International Society for Technology in Education (http://www.iste.org)

International Technology Education Association (http://www.iteawww.org)

International Teleconferencing Association (http://www.itca.org)

National Education Association (http://www.nea.org)

National Science Teachers Association (http://www.nsta.org)

Society for Applied Learning and Technology (http://www.salt.org)

U.S. Distance Learning Association (http://www.usdla.org)

Collections/Archives

Global School Net (http://www.gsn.org/teach/articles)

MCCCD Learning Communities (http://www.mcli.dist.maricopa.edu/
monograph/index.html)

MCREL Technology Integration (http://www.mcrel.org/resources/technol-
ogy/index.asp)

Living Schoolbook Project (http://lsb.syr.edu)

U.S. Department of Education, Office of Technology (http://www.ed.gov/Technology/pubsh.html)

Worldbank Worldlinks (http://www.worldbank.org/worldlinks)

Research Centers

Knowledge Media Institute, Open University (http://kmi.open.ac.uk)

Institute for Computer Based Learning, Heriot-Watt Unversity (http://www.icbl.hw.ac.uk)

Institute for Learning Sciences, Northwestern University (http://www.ils.nwu.edu)

Institute for Learning Technologies, Columbia University (http://www.ilt.columbia.edu)

National Center for Supercomputer Applications, University of Illinois (http://www.nsca.edu)

The Concord Consortium (http://www.concord.org)

Virtual Reality & Education Lab, East Carolina University (http://eastnet.educ.ecu.edu/vr/vrel.htm)

Networks

Consortium for School Networking (http://www.cosn.org)

Corporation for Research and Educational Networking (http://www.cren.net)

Cisco Educational Archive (http://www.cearch.org)

3Com Education (http://www.3com.com/edu)

Internet2 (http://www.internet2.org)

Internet Society (http://www.isoc.org)

WWW Virtual Library: Networking (http://src.doc.ic.ac.uk/bySubject/Networking.html)

Appendix:
Case Studies

Many examples of relevant and interesting Web sites have been provided throughout the book; this appendix describes a few exemplary ones in a little more depth. As always, readers are encouraged to examine the sites directly.

Maricopa Community Colleges

The Maricopa Community College District (MCCD) in Arizona is one of the nation's largest community college systems, encompassing ten colleges and serving more than 200,000 students. MCCD is not only one of the largest, but also one of the most technologically advanced. All aspects of MCCD operations are available online; a nice overview is provided by "One Connected Day at Maricopa" (see http://www.maricopa.edu/connect/index.htm). MCCD has a Vice-Chancellor of Information Technology—an indication that technology planning and operations are a critical element of college administration.

The main Web page for MCDD (http://www. maricopa.edu) allows easy access to all information about the colleges and course offerings.

The Maricopa Center for Learning and Instruction (MCLI) provides support to all college faculty, students, and staff in their efforts to use technology for learning and teaching. Its primary mission is to encourage innovation. Having such a center is vital to the ongoing success of technology at an educational institution.

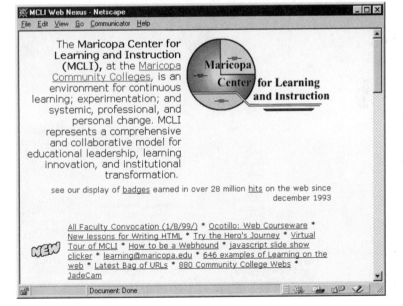

Boulder Valley School District

The Boulder Valley School District (BVSD) illustrates the increasing use of the Web/Internet by school districts around the country. BVSD includes thirty-four elementary schools, fourteen middle schools, and ten high schools in the Boulder, Colorado, area. The school district maintains the Web site, but each school takes care of its own Web pages—maintaining the local control and diversity that characterize the U.S. public education system.

The BVSD site provides information about the activities of the school board, school lunch menus, bus schedules, assessment test results, notices of job openings, details of the curriculum, professional development opportunities, learning/teaching resources, and documentation for using the Internet. BVSD is a participant in national and state computing initiatives and also partners with local corporations.

The Boulder Valley School District Web site (http://www.bvsd.k12. co.us) is typical of what school systems around the country are doing.

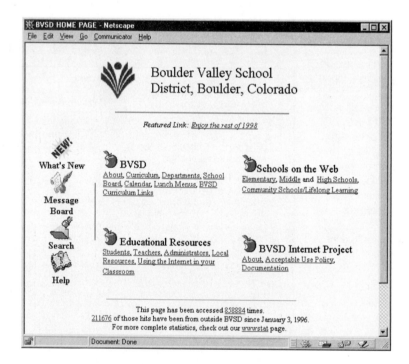

The Cyber Travel Specialist

An intriguing example of Web-based training is the Cyber Travel Specialist program developed by Internet Learning Systems and supported by the Institute of Certified Travel Agents and major hotel chains. The program, which describes itself as "Internet School for the Travel Professional," is a fifteen-lesson course on how to use the Internet for travel-related information. It includes an online certification test to verify that the student has achieved the competencies taught in the course.

The Cyber Travel Specialist program illustrates how online training courses developed by independent vendors can meet needs not addressed by current educational institutions.

The Cyber Travel Specialist (http://cybertravelspecialist.com) provides Internet training to travel professionals.

Motorola University

In the book, we discussed the development of corporate universities as a way that organizations can leverage their training and education resources (generate additional revenue). A good example is Motorola University (MU), which offers existing and customized courses on a broad range of topics to outside clients. Topic areas include management, sales, leadership, quality, engineering, manufacturing, and customer service.

Motorola University also includes a bookstore for ordering publications of Motorola University Press and other publications relevant to training. At the present time, the courses and services offered by MU are in-person, but over time more of them are likely to be done online—following the lead of academic institutions.

Motorola University (http://mu.motorola. com) provides a variety of training courses and services to outside clients.

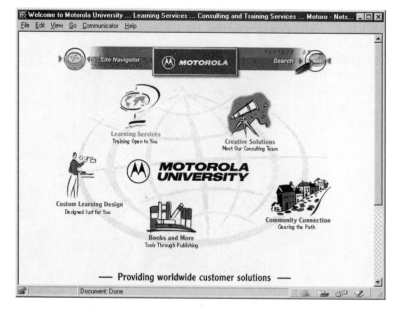

Tech Corps

Tech Corps is a nonprofit organization created to support technology in schools. Its mission is to recruit, place, and support volunteers from the technology community who advise and assist schools in the introduction and integration of new technologies; to bring additional technology resources to schools through local and national projects; and to build partnerships in support of educational technology among educators, businesses, and community members at the local, state, and national levels.

Tech Corps is currently active in forty-two states and has hundreds of volunteers helping schools with their technology activities. Sponsorship is provided by a number of corporations, associations, and foundations.

Tech Corps (http://www.ustc.org) is a nationwide organization of volunteers dedicated to helping schools use technology.

Chemistry: The Central Science

Even in the information age, textbooks play a critical role in learning. However, the textbooks of tomorrow are likely to be online, not printed. At the present time, we see a transition from print to online materials: Many textbooks have an accompanying online study guide. As an example, consider the Web site for *Chemistry: The Central Science* (7th edition) by Brown, Lemay, and Bursten, published by Prentice-Hall (http://www.prenhall.com/brown). This textbook is used by many college chemistry departments around the country (for example, Louisiana State University, http://www.chem.lsu.edu). Each chapter of the online guide includes problem-solving help (include practice tests), exercises based on current topics, visualization aids, explanations in RealAudio, and Web links to relevant sites.

The Cisco Network Academy

Information technologists who understand networks are in high demand and are likely to remain so in the future. It is difficult for schools to prepare students for such positions because they lack the expertise and equipment needed for training. It makes a lot of sense for network companies themselves to play a key role in such training. This is exactly what Cisco Systems, a major provider of network technology and services, has done with its Cisco Networking Academy. The academy consists of high schools and colleges around the country that are authorized by Cisco to teach a four-semester course on network, including a certification exam at the end (as a Cisco Certified Network Associate or Professional). The academy is organized into regional and local sites; the regional sites train and support the local sites, ensuring quality control of the program.

The Cisco Networking Academy is a nice example of an industry–education partnership that produces big payoffs for all involved (especially students).

The Cisco Networking Academy (http://www.cisco.com/edu/academies) provides training to students at high schools and colleges around the country. Successful completion of the course earns certification.

Moneyopolis

Moneyopolis is a financial planning game for kids in the sixth through eighth grades developed by the accounting firm Ernst & Young as a public service. The game involves making money in the virtual town of Moneyopolis. The site is designed to provide practice in basic math skills and problem solving; activities are correlated with NCTM standards and objectives. Lesson guides for teachers are provided, along with a library of relevant readings (articles from kids' magazines).

While some may view this site as self-serving (the basic financial model embodied in the game is a simple version of the one Ernst & Young uses with clients), it is a nice example of how the business world can contribute interesting and useful educational materials. Learning math skills in the context of money and financial planning is probably one of the more meaningful ways for kids to learn mathematics—and the game is fun, too!

Moneyopolis (http://www.moneyopolis.com) is a financial planning game for kids developed by Ernst & Young.

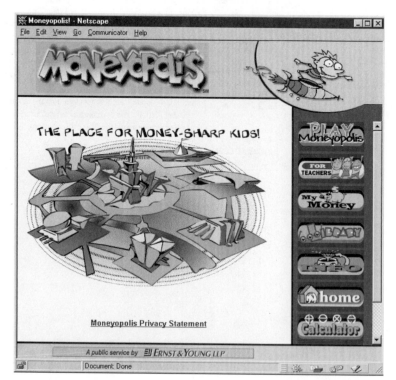

The History Channel

As any teacher can tell you, history is a difficult subject to teach. Although it should be a fascinating topic for all students, it is often perceived as boring and dull. However, when presented in the form of television programs and videos, it typically captures the attention and interest of most students.

The History Channel Web site is a useful tool for teachers and students. It makes the extensive resources of the television network available interactively. The site provides a continually changing series of featured stories and permits searching of the network's archives. All the information presented is tied to broadcasts or videos available for sale (it is a commercial site, after all). In the future, all video footage is likely to be available in digital form and downloadable in real time. This would really make the site valuable!

The History Channel Web site (http://www.historychannel.com) provides information tied into network broadcasts and available videos.

Kentucky Department of Education

State departments of education have many stakeholders to please: parents, school administrators, teachers, politicians. Keeping everyone informed about their activities and providing a way for all concerned to have input to the decision-making process are difficult. But the Web provides an ideal way to do both. The Kentucky Department of Education site illustrates how government agencies can function better through online interaction. Typical issues addressed include student achievement testing, new curriculum initiatives, professional development opportunities for teachers, improved school management, and parental involvement.

The Kentucky Department of Education Web site (http://www.kde.state.ky.us) is used to inform everyone interested in education in the state about new developments and to collect input for policymaking.

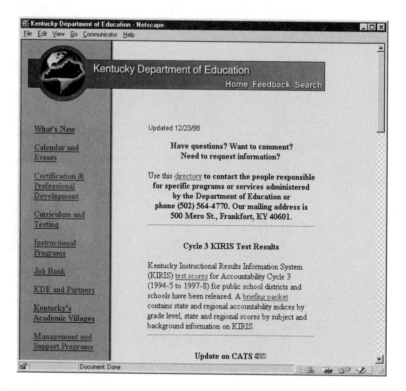

Tapped In

Throughout this book, we have emphasized the significance of networks for communication among students and educators. The Tapped In site created by SRI International is intended as an online "gathering place" for teachers. It provides a forum for ongoing discussions about issues of interest to teachers across the country, either in specific curriculum areas or on important general topics (such as school violence or school-based management). Most discussions are real-time and make use of MUDs.

The Tapped In site (http://www.tappedin.sri.com) provides a discussion forum for teachers.

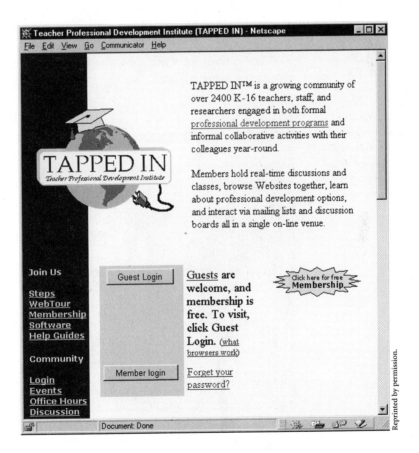

TAPPED IN™ is a growing community of over 2400 K-16 teachers, staff, and researchers engaged in both formal professional development programs and informal collaborative activities with their colleagues year-round.

Members hold real-time discussions and classes, browse Websites together, learn about professional development options, and interact via mailing lists and discussion boards all in a single on-line venue.

Guests are welcome, and membership is free. To visit, click Guest Login. (what browsers work)

Forget your password?

Reprinted by permission.

MAX @ SCHOOL

All of the previous examples have been products of institutions and organizations; the last example is an individual effort. MAX @ SCHOOL is a real-time adventure story about a four-year kayak trip from the west coast of Canada to the east coast via Nicaragua (the long way around)! Max (aka Corey Richardson) posts regular online journal entries along the way, with multimedia details of his trip. While this is clearly not anything like lessons from a textbook, it is rich in details of geography, sociology, athletics, and computer technology—as well as an interesting exercise in creative writing with worldwide online participation. Max also has established the STRATA Foundation to offer scholarships for high school students who would like to have similar learning experiences in the future.

This example may not seem very profound, but it conveys the true spirit of learning in cyberspace.

A living adventure novel: a kayak trip from one coast of Canada to the other via Nicaragua (http://www.solomax. com).

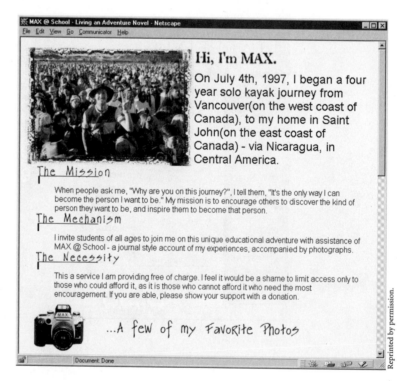

Glossary

asynchronous   interaction that takes place over time, such as email or discussion forums

audiographics   a form of synchronous conferencing that involves the simultaneous use of voice and computer screen sharing; may involve either one or two phone lines

bandwidth   the information-carrying capacity of a network connection, usually measured in terms of transmission speed (ranging from 14.4 kilobytes per second to more than 500 megabytes per second)

browser   program that allows access to the Web and reads HTML files (for example, Internet Explorer, Netscape Communicator)

CAI (computer-assisted instruction) or **CBI (computer-based instruction)**   traditional forms of computer-based learning that involve interaction with programs (instead of other people)

CD-ROM (compact disc–read only memory)   compact disc that can be used to store approximately 600 megabytes of data

chat   a form of synchronous conferencing that involves the exchange of text messages in a conversational manner

CSCW (computer-supported cooperative work)   hardware and software designed to facilitate online teamwork or group interaction

download   receive files from another computer

FAQs (frequently asked questions)   Web page(s) listing frequently asked questions along with responses

FTP (file transfer program)   program used to transfer files from one computer system to another

home page   the main (default) document that appears when a Web site is accessed

host   a computer that links up servers, PCs, and peripheral devices (such as printers and disk drives).

HTML (hypertext markup language)   the formatting language used for Web documents

Internet   a network of networks that all use the same TCP/IP transmission format

intranet   a private network of networks within an organization or institution

ISDN (integrated services digital network)   a relatively high speed (128 kilobytes per second) form of network connection provided by telecommunication companies

ISP (Internet service provider)   company that provides local Internet connections

IP (Internet protocol) address   the unique identifier for a computer on the Internet

LAN (local area network)   a private network that connects computers within a school or across a campus using cables or wireless links

modem   computer device that allows standard telephone lines (analog) to be connected to data (digital) networks

netiquette   conventions for online behavior

plug-in   a program that is added to a Web browser to provide additional capabilities (usually downloaded from the Web)

ports   input/output connections on a computer (for example, serial ports on a PC or dial-up ports on a host)

router   a special-purpose computer that handles network communication

server   a computer that serves as the hub for a network (LAN or WAN)

streaming media   the real-time delivery of multimedia presentations in small "bursts" using a program such as RealMedia

synchronous   interaction that takes place in real time, such as chats or video-conferences

T1   a high-speed data transmission line (usually 1.5 megabytes per second) provided by telecommunication companies

upload   send files to another computer

URL (universal resource locator)   Web address (for example, http://www.here.net)

WAN (wide area network)   a public network that connects systems over a broad geographical area (for example, the Internet)

References

Allessi, S., & Trollip, S. (1991). *Computer based instruction: Methods and development.* Englewood Cliffs, NJ: Prentice-Hall.

Anderson, T. (1996). The virtual conference: Extending professional education in cyberspace. *Intl J. Educ. Telecommunications, 2*(2/3), 121–135.

Angell, D., & Heslop, B. (1994). *The elements of e-mail style.* Reading, MA: Addison-Wesley.

Baker, E. L., & O'Neil, H. F. (1994). *Technology assessment in education and training.* Hillsdale, NJ: Erlbaum.

Barry, D. (1996). *Dave Barry in cyberspace.* New York: Ballantine.

Benedikt, M. (1991). *Cyberspace: First steps.* Cambridge, MA: MIT Press.

Benson, A. C, & Fodemski, L. (1996). *Connecting kids and the Internet: A handbook for librarians, teachers, and parents.* New York: Neal-Shuman.

Berge, Z. (1996). *The role of the online instructor/facilitator.* [http://star.ucc.nau.edu/~mauri/moderate/teach-online.html]

Berge, Z., & Collins, M. (Eds.). (1995). *Computer mediated communication and the online classroom (Vols. I–III).* Cresskill, NJ: Hampton Press.

Berge, Z., & Collins, M. (Eds.). (1996). *Wired together: The online K–12 classroom.* Cresskill, NJ: Hampton Press.

Bonk, C. J., & King, K. S. (Eds.). (1998). *Electronic collaborators: Learner-centered technologies for literacy, apprenticeship, and discourse.* Mahwah, NJ: Erlbaum.

Bothun, G. D., & Kevan, S. D. (1996, July/August). *Networked physics in undergraduate instruction: Computers in physics.* [http://zebu.oregon.edu/special/cip.html]

Bowers, C. A. (1988). *The cultural dimensions of educational technology: Understanding the non-neutrality of technology.* New York: Teachers College Press.

Boyle, T., & Boyle, T. (1996). *Design for multimedia learning.* New York: Prentice-Hall.

Briggs, L. J., Gustafson, K. L., & Tillman, M. H. (1991). *Instructional design: Principles and applications.* Englewood Cliffs, NJ: Educational Technology Publications.

Brown, B. M. (1998). Digital classrooms: Some myths about developing new education programs using the internet. *THE Journal.*

Brown, J. S., Collins, A., & Duguid, P. (1996). Situated cognition and the culture of learning. In H. McLellan (Ed.), *Situated learning perspectives.* Englewood Cliffs, NJ: Educational Technology Publications.

Campbell, D., & Campbell, M. (1995). *The student's guide to doing research on the Internet.* Reading, MA: Addison-Wesley.

Carroll, J. (1990). *The Nurnberg funnel.* Cambridge, MA: MIT Press.

Carroll, J. (1998). *Minimalism: Beyond the Nurnberg funnel.* Cambridge, MA: MIT Press.

Cavazos, E. A., & Morin, G. (1994). *Cyberspace and the law: Your rights and duties in the online world.* Cambridge, MA: MIT Press.

Coleman, D. (1997). *Groupware: Collaborative strategies for corporate LANs and intranets.* Englewood Cliffs, NJ: Prentice-Hall.

Collis, B. (1996). *Tele-Learning in a digital world.* London: International Thomson Computer Press.

Cook, A., & Hussey, S. (1995). *Assistive technologies: Principles and practice.* St. Louis: Mosby.

Coombs, N., & Cunningham, C. (1997). *Information access and adaptive technology.* Phoenix, AZ: Oryx Press.

Covington, G., & Hannah, B. (1996). *Access by design.* New York: Van Nostrand Reinhold.

Cox, B. (1996). Evolving a distributed learning community. In Z. Berge & M. Collins (Eds.), *Wired together: The online K–12 classroom.* Cresskill, NJ: Hampton Press.

Cross, P. (1981). *Adults as learners.* San Francisco: Jossey-Bass.

Crouch, M. L., & Montecino, V. (1997). *Cyberstress: Asynchronous anxiety, or worried in cyberspace: I wonder if my teacher got my email.* [http://leahi.kcc.hawaii.edu/org/tcc-conf/pres/crouch.html]

Cuban, L. (1986). *Teachers and machines: The classroom use of technology since 1920.* New York: Teachers College Press.

Cummins, J., & Sayers, D. (1995). *Brave new schools: Challenging cultural illiteracy through global learning networks.* New York: St. Martin's Press.

Davenport, T. (1997). *Information ecology.* New York: Oxford.

Davidow, W. H., & Malone, M. S. (1992). *The virtual corporation.* New York: Harper Business.

Dede, C. (1996). Emerging technologies and distributed learning. *American Journal of Distance Education, 10*(2), 4–36.

Denning, D., & Denning, P. (1998). *Internet besieged.* Reading, MA: Addison-Wesley.

Dertouzos, M. (1997). *What will be.* New York: Harper Edge.

Dick, W., & Carey, L. (1990). *The systematic design of instruction.* Glenview, IL: Scott, Foresman.

Dizard, W. (1997). *Meganet: How the global communications network will connect everyone on earth.* Boulder, CO: Westview Press.

Doheny-Farina, S. (1996). *The wired neighborhood.* New Haven: Yale University Press.

Dreyfus, H. (1992). *What computers (still) can't do.* Cambridge, MA: MIT Press.

Druin, A. (1999). *The design of children's technology.* San Francisco: Morgan Kaufman.

Druin, A., & Solomon, C. (1996). *Designing multimedia environments for children.* New York: Wiley.

Duchastel, P. (1996/97). A Web-based model for university instruction. *Journal of Educational Technology Systems, 25*(3), 221–228. [http://fcae.nova.edu/~duchaste]

Duning, B., Van Kekerix, B., & Zabrowski, L. (1993). *Reaching learners through telecommunications.* San Francisco: Jossey-Bass.

Dunlop, C., & Kling, R. (1996). *Computers and controversy* (2nd ed.). Boston: Academic Press.

Eastmond, D. V. (1995). *Alone but together: Adult distance study through computer conferencing.* Cresskill, NJ: Hampton Press.

Edelson, D., Pea, R., & Gomez, L. (1996). Constructivism in the collaboratory. In. B. G. Wilson (Ed.), *Constructivist learning environments.* Englewood Cliffs, NJ: Educational Technology Publications.

Farr, M., & Psotka, J. (1992). *Intelligent instruction by computer.* Washington: Taylor & Francis.

Feenberg, A. (1991). *Critical theory of technology.* New York: Oxford University Press.

Fisher, C., Dwyer, D. C., & Yokam, K. (1996*). Education & technology: Reflections on computing in classrooms.* San Francisco: Jossey-Bass.

Furger, R. (1998). *Does Jane compute? Preserving our daughters' place in the cyber revolution.* New York: Warner Books.

Galitz, W. O. (1997). *The essential guide to user interface design.* New York: Wiley.

Garner, R., & Gillingham, M. (1996). *Internet communication in six classrooms: Conversations across time, space and culture.* Mahwah, NJ: Erlbaum.

Gascoyne, R. J., & Ozcubucku, K. (1996). *The corporate Internet planning guide.* New York: Van Nostrand Reinhold.

Gibbons, A., & Fairweather, P. (1998). *Designing computer based instruction.* Englewood Cliffs, NJ: Educational Technology Publications.

Gibson, W. (1984). *Neuromancer.* New York: Ace.

Hannum, W., & Hansen, C. (1989). *Instructional systems development in large organizations.* Englewood Cliffs, NJ: Educational Technology Publications.

Harasim, L. (1990). *Online education: Perspectives on a new environment.* New York: Praeger.

Harasim, L. (1993). *Global networks: Computers and international communication.* Cambridge, MA: MIT Press.

Harasim, L., Hiltz, S. R., Teles, L., & Turoff, M. (1995). *Learning networks: A field guide to teaching and learning online.* Cambridge, MA: MIT Press.

Hartman, K., et al. (1995). Patterns of social interaction and learning to write: Some effects of network technologies. In Z. Berge & M. Collins (Eds.), *Computer mediated education and the online classroom.* Cresskill, NJ: Hampton Press.

Hauben, M., & Hauben, R. (1997). *Netizens.* Los Alamitos, CA: IEEE Computer Society Press.

Hazemi, R., Hailes, S., & Wilbur, S. (1998). *The digital university.* New York: Springer.

Healy, J. (1998). *Failure to connect: How computers affect our children's minds.* New York: Simon & Schuster.

Hiltz, S. R. (1994). *The virtual classroom: Learning without limits via computer networks.* Norwood, NJ: Ablex.

Hiltz, S. R., & Turoff, M. (1993). *The network nation: Human communication via computer* (rev. ed.). Cambridge, MA: MIT Press.

Hix, D., & Hartson, H. R. (1995). *Developing user interfaces.* New York: Wiley & Sons.

Howlett, V. (1995). *Visual interface design.* New York: Wiley & Sons.

Ingebritsen, T. S., & Flickinger, K. (1998*). Development and assessment of Web courses that use streaming audio and video technologies.* Annual Conference on Distance Teaching and Learning, Madison, WI.

Jackson, S. (1997). *Beyond Web course design: Designing online dialogue.* NAU Web 97 Conference. [http://star.ucc.nau.edu/~nauweb97/papers/jackson1.html]

Jones, S. G. (1995). *Cybersociety.* Newbury Park, CA: Sage.

Jonnasen, D. H. (1996). *Handbook of research on educational communications and technology.* New York: Macmillan.

Kaye, A. (1992). *Collaborative learning through computer conferencing.* New York: Springer-Verlag.

Kearsley, G. (1994). *Public access systems.* Englewood Cliffs, NJ: Ablex.

Kearsley, G., Hunter, B., & Furlong, M. (1992). *We teach with technology.* Wilsonville, OR: Franklin, Beedle.

Kearsley, G., Lynch, W., & Wizer, D. (1995). The effectiveness and impact of computer conferencing in graduate education. [http://www.gww.edu/~etl/cmc.html]

Kearsley, G., & Shneiderman, B. (1998). Engagement theory. *Educational Technology, 38*(3). [http://home.sprynet.com/~gkearsley/engage.htm]

Khan, B. (1997). *Web-based instruction.* Englewood Cliffs, NJ: Educational Technology Publications. [http://www.gwu.edu/~etlalex/khan/tc.txt]

Knowles, M. (1978). *The adult learner.* Houston: Gulf Publishing.

Kommers, P. (1996). *Hypermedia learning environments: Instructional design and integration.* Hillsdale, NJ: Erlbaum.

Landauer, T. (1995). *The trouble with computers.* Cambridge, MA: MIT Press.

Lave, J., & Wenger, E. (1990). *Situated learning.* Cambridge, UK: Cambridge University Press.

Lazzaro, J. (1996) *Adapting PCs for disabilities.* Reading, MA: Addison-Wesley.

Leonard, G. (1968*). Education and ecstasy.* New York: Dell.

Leshin, C. B. (1996). *Internet adventures: Step-by-step guide for finding and using educational resources.* Boston: Allyn & Bacon.

Leshin, C. B., Pollock, J., & Reigeluth, C. M. (1992). *Instructional design strategies and tactics.* Englewood Cliffs, NJ: Educational Technology Publications.

Levin, J., et al. (1989). Observations on educational networks: The importance of appropriate activities for learning. *The Computing Teacher, 16,* 32–39. [http://lrs.ed.ucic.edu/Guidelines/LRWS.htm]

Levinson, P. (1997*). The soft edge: A natural history and future of the information revolution.* London: Routledge.

Lipnack, J., & Stamps, J. (1997*). Virtual teams: Reaching across space-time and organizations with technology.* New York: Wiley. [http://www.netage.com]

Lombardo, N. (1996). *Internet Navigator: Final report.* Salt Lake City: University of Utah.

Ludlow, P. (1996). *High noon on the electronic frontier: Conceptual issues in cyberspace.* Cambridge, MA: MIT Press.

Maddux, C., Johnson, D., & Willis, J. (1997). *Educational computing* (2nd ed.). Boston: Allyn & Bacon.

Marquardt, M., & Kearsley, G. (1999). *Technology-based learning.* Boca Raton, FL: St. Lucie Press/ASTD.

Martin, C. (1999). *NetFuture: The seven cybertrends that will drive business, create new wealth, and define your future.* New York: McGraw-Hill.

Martin, J. (1996). *Cybercorp.* New York: AmaCom.

McCormack, C., & Jones, D. (1997). *Building a Web-Based education system.* New York: Wiley.

Means, B., et al. (1995). Beyond the classroom: Restructuring schools with technology. *Phi Delta Kappan, 77*(1), 69–72. [http://www.ed.gov/Technology/pubs.html]

Miller, S. (1996). *Civilizing cyberspace.* Reading, MA: Addison-Wesley.

Minoli, D. (1996*). Distance learning technology and applications.* Boston: Artech House.

Molnar, A. (1997). Computers in education: A brief history. *THE Journal, 24*(11), 63–68.

Moore, M., & Kearsley, G. (1996). *Distance education: A systems approach.* Belmont, CA: Wadsworth.

Moreinis, B. (1996). *Time, space, and culture in school computer development initiatives.* [http://www.ilt.columbia.edu/k12/livetext/readings/index.html]

Negroponte, N. (1995*). Being digital.* New York: Knopf.

Neumann, P. (1995). *Computer related risks.* New York: ACM Press/Addison-Wesley.

Norman, D. (1993). *Things that make us smart.* Reading, MA: Addison-Wesley.

O'Neil, H. F. (1979). *Procedures for instructional systems development.* New York: Academic Press.

Palloff, R., & Pratt, K. (1999). *Building learning communities in cyberspace.* San Francisco: Jossey-Bass.

Papert, S. (1980). *Mindstorms.* New York: Basic Books.

Papert S. (1993). *The children's machine: Rethinking school in the age of the computer.* New York: Basic Books.

Papert. S. (1996). *The connected family: Bridging the digital generation gap.* Atlanta: Longstreet Press.

Paulsen, M. F. (1995). Moderating educational computer conferences. In Z. Berge & M. Collins Eds.), *Computer mediated communication and the online.* Cresskill, NJ: Hampton Press.

Perelman, L. (1992). *School's out.* New York: Avon.

Porter, L. R. (1997). *Creating the virtual classroom: Distance learning with the Internet.* New York: Wiley.

Postman, N. (1992*). Technopoly.* New York: Knopf.

Poulson, M., & Richardson, J. (1988). *Foundations of intelligent tutoring systems.* Hillsdale, NJ: Erlbaum.

Reddick, R., & King, E. (1996). *The online student.* Orlando, FL: Harcourt Brace College Publishers.

Rheingold, H. (1991). *Virtual reality.* New York: Simon & Schuster.

Rheingold, H. (1993). *The virtual community.* Reading, MA: Addison-Wesley.

Riel, M., & Levin, J. (1990). Building electronic communities: Success and failure in computer networking. *Instructional Science, 19,* 145–169.

Rosenberg, R. (1997). *The social impact of computers* (2nd ed.). San Diego: Academic Press.

Rossman, P. (1992). *The emerging worldwide electronic university: Information age global higher education.* Westport, CT: Greenwood Press.

Ruberg, L. F., Taylor, C. D., & Moore, D. M. (1996). Student participation and interaction on-line: A case study of two college classes: Freshman writing and a plant science lab. *Intl J. of Educational Telecommunications, 2*(1), 69–92.

Schank, R. (1997). *Virtual learning.* New York: McGraw-Hill.

Schon, D. A. (1990). *Educating the reflective practitioner.* San Francisco: Jossey-Bass.

Schrage, M. (1991). *Shared minds: The new technologies of collaboration.* New York: Random House.

Schrum, L., & Berenfeld, B. (1997). *Teaching and learning in the information age: A guide to educational telecommunications.* Boston: Allyn & Bacon.

Shaw, R. (1996). *The FAQ manual of style.* Cambridge, MA: MIT Press.

Shea, V. (1994). *Netiquette.* San Francisco: Albion.

Sherry, L. (1997, September). The Boulder Valley Internet Project: Lessons learned. *THE Journal,* 68–72. [http://www.cudenver.edu/~lsherry/pubs/bvip97.html]

Shneiderman, B. (1998). *Designing the user interface* (3rd ed). Reading, MA: Addison Wesley Longman.

Smolan, R., & Erwitt, J. (1996). *24 hours in cyberspace.* New York: Random House.

Sproull, L., & Kiesler, S. (1991). *Connections: New ways of working in the networked organization.* Cambridge, MA: MIT Press.

Steen, D. R., Roddy, M. R., Sheffield, D., & Stout, M. B. (1995). *Teaching with the Internet.* Bellevue, WA: Resolution Press.

Stefik, M. (1997). *Internet dreams.* Cambridge, MA: MIT Press.

Strate, P. L., Jacobson, R., & Gibson, S. (1996). *Communication and cyberspace: Social interaction in an electronic environment.* Cresskill, NJ: Hampton.

Szuprowicz, B. O. (1995). *Multimedia networks.* New York: McGraw-Hill.

Tapscott, D. (1997). *The digital economy.* New York: McGraw-Hill.

Tinker, R., & Haavind, S. (1996). Netcourses and netseminars: Current practice and new designs. *Journal of Science Education and Technology, 5*(3), 217–223. [http://www.concord.org/pubs/model.html]

Towne, D. (1995). *Learning and instruction in simulation environments.* Englewood Cliffs, NJ: Educational Technology Publications.

Turkle, S. (1995). *Life on the screen: Identity in the age of the Internet.* New York: Simon & Schuster.

Waggonner, M. D. (1992). *Empowering networks: Computer conferencing in education.* Englewood Cliffs, NJ: Educational Technology Press.

Warschauer, M. (1998). *Electronic literacies: Language, culture and power in online education.* Mahwah, NJ: Erlbaum.

Whittle, D. (1997). *Cyberspace: The human dimension.* San Francisco: W.H. Freeman.

Williams, B. (1995). *The Internet for teachers.* Indianapolis: IDG Books.

Yager, R. (1991, September). The constructivist learning model. *The Science Teacher,* pp. 52–57.

Young, K. (1998). *Caught in the Net.* New York: Wiley & Sons.

Index